Nāgārjuna's Guide
to
The Bodhisattva Path

The publication of this book has been enabled by
a generous donation from Sunny Lou.

Nāgārjuna's Guide
to
The Bodhisattva Path

Ārya Nāgārjuna's
Treatise on the Provisions for Enlightenment
(Bodhisaṃbhāra Śāstra)

With a Selective Abridgement of Bhikshu Vaśitva's Early Indian
Bodhisaṃbhāra Śāstra Commentary

Translation, Abridgement & Explanatory Notes
By Bhikshu Dharmamitra

Kalavinka Press
Seattle, Washington
WWW.KALAVINKAPRESS.ORG

KALAVINKA PRESS
8603 39th Ave SW
Seattle, WA 98136 USA

WWW.KALAVINKAPRESS.ORG / WWW.KALAVINKA.ORG

Kalavinka Press is the publishing arm of the Kalavinka Dharma Association, a non-profit organized exclusively for religious educational purposes as allowed within the meaning of section 501(c)3 of the Internal Revenue Code. KDA was founded in 1990 and gained formal approval in 2004 by the United States Internal Revenue Service as a 501(c)3 non-profit organization to which donations are tax deductible.

Donations to KDA are accepted by mail and on the Kalavinka website where numerous free Dharma translations and excerpts from Kalavinka publications are available in digital format.

Edition: BsamEZ-SA-0408-1.0

ISBN: 978-1-935413-02-8
Library of Congress Control Number: 2009920870

PUBLISHER'S CATALOGING-IN-PUBLICATION DATA

Nagarjuna, 2nd c.
[Puti ziliang lun / Bodhisaṃbhāra Shastra. English translation.]
Nagarjuna's Guide to the Bodhisattva Path. Arya Nagarjuna's Treatise on the Provisions for Enlightenment. With a Selective Abridgement of Bhikshu Vaśitva's Early Indian Bodhisaṃbhāra Shastra Commentary.
Translation and abridgement by Bhikshu Dharmamitra. – 1st ed. – Seattle, WA: Kalavinka Press, 2009.
p. ; cm.
ISBN: 978-1-935413-02-8
Includes: stanza directory; commentary abridgement; facing-page Chinese source text in both traditional and simplified scripts.
Other Authors: Bhikshu Vaśitva; Bhikshu Dharmamitra.
1. Bodhisattvas. 2. Spiritual life—Mahayana Buddhism. I. Vaśitva, Bhikshu. *ca* 2nd–4th c. II. Dharmamitra, Bhikshu. 1948– . III. Title.

2009920870
0902

Cover and interior designed and composed by Bhikshu Dharmamitra.

Dedicated to the memory of the selfless and marvelous life of the Venerable Dhyāna Master Hsuan Hua, the Weiyang Ch'an Patriarch and the very personification of the Bodhisattva Path.

DHYĀNA MASTER HSUAN HUA

宣化禪師

1918–1995

CONTENTS

DIRECTORY BY VERSE TO COMMENTARY DISCUSSIONS
(One-line verse synopses and section titles composed by the translator.)

ACKNOWLEDGMENTS

The accuracy and readability of of these first ten books of translations have been significantly improved with the aid of extensive corrections, preview comments, and editorial suggestions generously contributed by Bhikkhu Bodhi, Jon Babcock, Timothy J. Lenz, Upasaka Feng Ling, Upāsaka Guo Ke, Upāsikā Min Li, and Richard Robinson. Additional valuable editorial suggestions and corrections were offered by Bhikshu Huifeng and Bruce Munson.

The publication of the initial set of ten translation volumes has been assisted by substantial donations to the Kalavinka Dharma Association by Bill and Peggy Brevoort, Freda Chen, David Fox, Upāsaka Guo Ke, Chenping and Luther Liu, Sunny Lou, Jimi Neal, and "Leo L." (*Camellia sinensis folium*). Additional donations were offered by Doug Adams, Diane Hodgman, Bhikshu Huifeng, Joel and Amy Lupro, Richard Robinson, Ching Smith, and Sally and Ian Timm.

Were it not for the ongoing material support provided by my late guru's Dharma Realm Buddhist Association and the serene translation studio provided by Seattle's Bodhi Dhamma Center, creation of this translation would have been immensely more difficult.

Most importantly, it would have been impossible for me to produce this translation without the Dharma teachings provided by my late guru, the Weiyang Ch'an Patriarch, Dharma teacher, and exegete, the Venerable Master Hsuan Hua.

ABBREVIATIONS, CITATIONS & ROMANIZATION PROTOCOLS

AV: Abridged Bhikshu Vaśitva Commentary

TN: Translator's Notes

Kalavinka Press *Taisho* citation style adds text numbers after volume numbers and before page numbers to assist rapid CBETA digital searches.

Romanization, where used, is Pinyin with the exception of names and terms already well-recognized in Wade-Giles.

THE CHINESE TEXT

This translation is supplemented by inclusion of Chinese source text on verso pages in both traditional and simplified scripts. Taisho-supplied variant readings from other editions are presented as Chinese endnotes.

This Chinese text and its variant readings are from the April, 2004 version of the Chinese Buddhist Electronic Text Association's digital edition of the Taisho compilation of the Buddhist canon.

Those following the translation in the Chinese should be aware that Taisho scripture punctuation is not traceable to original editions, is often erroneous and misleading, and is probably best ignored altogether. (In any case, accurate reading of Classical Chinese does not require any punctuation at all.)

INTRODUCTION

The Text and the Origins of This Translation

Ārya Nāgārjuna's *Treatise on the Provisions for Enlightenment* (*Bodhisaṃbhāra Śāstra*) together with its commentary by the Indian Bhikshu Vaśitva was translated into Chinese by the South Indian Tripiṭaka Master Dharmagupta in or around 609 CE in China's Sui Dynasty Capital. The two works are presented in interwoven format in the six-fascicle edition preserved in the Taisho compilation of the Chinese Buddhist canon (T32.1660.517b–41b). Neither the treatise nor the commentary are extant in either Sanskrit or Tibetan. As an important work by Ārya Nāgārjuna, it is a Dharma jewel well worth bringing forth for the benefit of Western Buddhists.

There have been no previous attempts to produce a literal English translation of Nāgārjuna's *Bodhisaṃbhāra Treatise* of which I am aware. In December, 2004, during a getaway to my retreat cabin on the Oregon coast, I finally found time to closely study this text. I remember being deeply pleased by the way in which this work gathered together all of the beautiful essentials of bodhisattva resolve, multi-lifetime vision, and altruistic practice into a relatively short, accessible, and comprehensive guide to the Bodhisattva Path.

I was doubly pleased to find that the very terse *ślokas* of this treatise were interwoven with a detailed, line-by-line explanatory commentary by an Indian monk who apparently lived not long after Ārya Nāgārjuna's life in the first quarter of the first millennium. The availability of such a fine commentary was especially fortuitous because it so nicely resolved the ambiguities encountered when contemplating the meaning of the treatise text proper.

Given the nature of this work's contents, I felt that the text deserved a clear and accurate English edition and so proceeded straightaway to produce a first-draft translation of the entire six-fascicle treatise and commentary.

Relying on multiple instances of internal evidence in the commentary, I have provisionally reconstructed the author's name as "Bhikshu Vaśitva." The nature of that evidence is detailed in the introduction to my complete translation of this commentary published under separate cover.

Special Features of the *Bodhisaṃbhāra Śāstra*

The especially attractive and useful features of this treatise lie in
its clear description of the essentials of the path to buddhahood,
including specific details about prerequisites to be fulfilled, frames
of mind and behaviors to be adopted or relinquished, the means for
accumulation of the two primary provisions consisting of merit and
wisdom, the means for overcoming karmic obstacles, the means to
be used in attracting beings to the Path, and the means to be used in
teaching Dharma to beings at every level of faith, intelligence, and
affinity, all in a relatively short treatise easily read, easily reviewed,
and amenable through its brevity to memorization.

The Relationship of this Treatise to Other Works of Nāgārjuna

This treatise is closely related in content to much longer works
by Nāgārjuna such as the *Strand of Jewels* (*Ratnāvalī*) and the *Ten
Grounds Vibhāṣā* (*Daśabhūmika Vibhāṣā*). Its relationship with the latter is particularly close as evidenced by the fact that the work on
the ten bodhisattva grounds repeatedly quotes both directly and
indirectly from this *Bodhisaṃbhāra Treatise.*

Unlike some other works attributed to the author of the *Middle
Treatise*, there seems to be no particular controversy about the
"original" Nāgārjuna's authorship of this work, this due to a relative abundance of internal and external evidence supporting the
relationship. The nature of the internal evidence lies primarily in
identity of doctrine discussed, identity of interpretive stance, identity of tone and aspirational tenor, and direct citation of classically
Nāgārjunian interpretive formulae.

On the Decision to Create an "Abridged" Edition of the Commentary

The extremely terse *ślokas* comprising this text are so metaphysi-
cally rich and replete with hidden meanings that anyone wishing to absorb Ārya Nāgārjuna's intent in writing the treatise will
require some sort of authoritative explanatory apparatus. To this
end, I translated the entire early Indian commentary by Bhikshu
Vaśitva at the same time that I first translated the treatise text.

But even Bhikshu Vaśitva's fine and detailed commentary has
limitations in terms of its suitability for a readership comprised
of individuals with such varying backgrounds as one encounters
among Western students and practitioners of Mahāyāna Buddhism.
Although the full-length commentary, graced with adequate

annotation, serves fairly well the needs of doctrine-obsessed monastics, scholars, and elite lay practitioners, the larger community of lay Buddhists would be bound to encounter difficulties with the length, complexity, and indirect style of Bhikshu Vaśitva's commentary.

This "variable-readership" reality suggested to me that, in releasing the treatise translation, I was facing a problem requiring a "middle-way" solution somewhere between simply publishing the easily misunderstood unadorned text and publishing the treatise in tandem with a long and sometimes rather abstruse commentary. The result of deliberating on this matter is the stratagem adopted in the current volume wherein the most crucially relevant passages from the long commentary are abridged, paraphrased, or summarized and then appended to each *śloka*. These are then each followed in turn, where helpful or necessary, by "optional reading" in the form of "translator's notes" contributing additional material useful to understanding the text.

On the Limitations of This Abridgement of the Indian Commentary

I hasten to point out the limitations of this abridgement of Bhikshu Vaśitva's fine early Indian commentary, as follows:

First, this condensation is both radical and selective and hence not at all rigorous in comprehensiveness of content. Although I attempted to refrain from excluding any primary doctrinal points, it might still be that crucially important ideas were left out.

Second, this abridgement of Bhikshu Vaśitva's commentary is recorded mostly in my words, not his. Thus any stylistic nuance attributable to the original author which might have survived the work's translation from Sanskrit to Chinese is erased in this condensation effort.

Due to the shortcomings of this radical abridgement, I encourage readers open to the detail of a comprehensive line-by-line explanation to prefer my translation of the unabridged commentary.

On the Translator's Explanatory Notes Included in This Volume

I feel that the translator's explanatory notes are required to explain important ideas and contribute doctrinal material not covered to any appreciable degree in either Ārya Nāgārjuna's text or Bhikshu Vaśitva's commentary. The need for the notes is occasioned by the fact that both the treatise text and commentary assume a solid familiarity with often very specific details of Buddhist texts and doctrines. Unfortunately, most modern students of Dharma simply do not possess such a fully ripened background. To expect that they might is simply not reasonable, this because much of the foundational material is not so readily available in English.

Some "translator's notes" contain directly-relevant supplemental information which I have translated from elsewhere in the Canon. Even though these "reference materials" are sometimes rather lengthy, I felt it best to include them in the notes rather than to exile them to appendices.

I hope the reader will forgive the inclusion of such broadly-ranging notes intended to clarify and amplify the meaning of the text. For those readers already familiar with the ideas covered in any particular "translator's note," there is certainly no reason not to simply skip right over to the next treatise *śloka*, focusing exclusively on the abridged commentary of Bhikshu Vaśitva.

On the Structure of This Volume

I have chosen to arrange the structure this volume's content according to the following schema:

1) To facilitate ready reference to any given *śloka*, following upon the brief general table of contents, I have included an additional relatively detailed table of contents consisting of my single-line summary of each *śloka*'s subject matter. (These "single-line summaries" are by no means definitive. They are simply a provisional didactic stratagem intended to facilitate study of the treatise.)

2) Next, I have set out the entire English translation of Ārya Nāgārjuna's treatise completely free of any potentially prejudicial outlining, *śloka* titling, or other interpretive apparatus. I have included both traditional and simplified Chinese text on the verso pages, this to assist more nuanced understanding of the text by those competent to read Sino-Buddhist classical Chinese.

3) Following on the presentation of the entire unadorned treatise text, each treatise *śloka* is set out yet again, preceded by a summarizing heading and followed by a paraphrasing abridgement of the relevant section of the Bhikshu Vaśitva commentary (signaled by "AV:"), and then by "translator's notes" (signaled by "TN:"). Some of the *śloka*s are already so clear that no translator's notes are included.

In Summation

As with nearly all translations of moderately technical classic Buddhist texts, there is certainly room for improvement in my efforts here on behalf of Ārya Nāgārjuna's treatise. Clergy, specialists, or Dharma students encountering errors, opacities, or infelicities are encouraged to send along any constructive suggestions for second-edition refinements via the Kalavinka Press website's email. I will be grateful for any such kindnesses bestowed and will give each suggestion close consideration for integration into subsequent editions.

I hope that this translation of Ārya Nāgārjuna's *Treatise on the Provisions for Enlightenment* together with the abridged Bhikshu Vaśitva commentary discussions and explanatory translator's notes will be useful to students and practitioners of the Bodhisattva Path.

Bhikshu Dharmamitra,
December, 2007

PART ONE:

THE TREATISE ON THE PROVISIONS
FOR ENLIGHTENMENT

Ārya Nāgārjuna's
BODHISAṂBHĀRA ŚĀSTRA

菩提資糧論 / 菩提资粮论

菩提資糧論 — 菩提资粮论

繁體字	简体字
菩提資糧論	**菩提资粮论**
聖者龍樹本 比丘自在釋	圣者龙树本 比丘自在释
大隋南印度三藏達磨笈多譯	大隋南印度三藏达磨笈多译
001 今於諸佛所合掌而頂敬 我當如教說佛菩提資糧	001 今于诸佛所合掌而顶敬 我当如教说佛菩提资粮
002 何能說無闕菩提諸資糧 唯獨有諸佛別得無邊覺	002 何能说无阙菩提诸资粮 唯独有诸佛别得无边觉
003 佛體無邊德覺資糧為根 是故覺資糧亦無有邊際	003 佛体无边德觉资粮为根 是故觉资粮亦无有边际
004 當說彼少分敬禮佛菩薩 是諸菩薩等次佛應供養	004 当说彼少分敬礼佛菩萨 是诸菩萨等次佛应供养
005 既為菩薩母亦為諸佛母 般若波羅蜜是覺初資糧	005 既为菩萨母亦为诸佛母 般若波罗蜜是觉初资粮

繁體字   简体字

THE TREATISE ON
THE PROVISIONS FOR ENLIGHTENMENT

The Bodhisaṃbhāra Śāstra
By Ārya Nāgārjuna

Translated into Chinese by the Great Sui Dynasty's
South Indian Tripiṭaka Master Dharmagupta (550?–619 CE)

001

Now, in the presence of all the Buddhas,
With palms pressed together, I bow down my head in reverence.
I shall explain here in accordance with the teachings
The provisions essential for the bodhi of the Buddhas.

002

How would one be able to describe without omission
All of the provisions for the realization of bodhi?
This could only be accomplished by the Buddhas themselves,
For they, exclusively, have realized the boundless enlightenment.

003

The boundless qualities of a buddha's body
Are rooted in the provisions essential to enlightenment.
Therefore the provisions for enlightenment
Themselves have no bounds.

004

I shall then explain but a lesser portion of them.
I render reverence to the Buddhas and the Bodhisattvas.
It is all such bodhisattvas as these
To whom one should next make offerings, after the Buddhas.

005

Since it is the mother of the Bodhisattvas,
It is also the mother of the Buddhas:
The prajñāpāramitā
Is foremost among the provisions essential for enlightenment.

006

施戒忍進定及此五之餘
皆由智度故波羅蜜所攝

007

此六波羅蜜總菩提資糧
猶如虛空中盡攝於諸物

008

復有餘師意諸覺資糧者
實捨及寂智四處之所攝

009

大悲徹骨髓為諸眾生依
如父於一子慈則遍一切

010

若念佛功德及聞佛神變
愛喜而受淨此名為大喜

011

菩薩於眾生不應得捨棄
當隨力所堪一切時攝受

012

菩薩從初時應隨堪能力
方便化眾生令入於大乘

006

施戒忍进定及此五之馀
皆由智度故波罗蜜所摄

007

此六波罗蜜总菩提资粮
犹如虚空中尽摄于诸物

008

复有馀师意诸觉资粮者
实舍及寂智四处之所摄

009

大悲彻骨髓为诸众生依
如父于一子慈则遍一切

010

若念佛功德及闻佛神变
爱喜而受净此名为大喜

011

菩萨于众生不应得舍弃
当随力所堪一切时摄受

012

菩萨从初时应随堪能力
方便化众生令入于大乘

繁體字　　　　　　　　簡体字

006

Because giving, moral virtue, patience, vigor, meditation,
And the others following from these five
All arise from the perfection of wisdom,
They are included within the pāramitās.

007

These six pāramitās
Encompass the provisions essential for bodhi,
They are comparable in this to empty space
Which entirely envelopes all things.

008

There is also the idea proposed by another master
That, as for the provisions for enlightenment,
Truth, relinquishment, cessation, and wisdom—
These four bases subsume them all.

009

The great compassion penetrates to the marrow of one's bones.
Thus one serves as a refuge for every being.
With a feeling as strong as a father's regard for his only son,
One's kindness extends universally to all beings.

010

If one brings to mind the qualities of a buddha
Or hears of a buddha's spiritual transformations,
One becomes purified through one's admiration and joyfulness.
This is what is meant by the great sympathetic joy.

011

In his relations with beings, the bodhisattva
Should not allow himself to forsake them.
As befits the abilities determined by his powers,
He should always strive to draw them in.

012

From the very beginning, the bodhisattva
Should accord with the power of his abilities
And use skillful means to instruct beings,
Causing them to enter the Great Vehicle.

013

化恒沙眾生令得羅漢果
化一入大乘此福德為上

014

教以聲聞乘及獨覺乘者
以彼少力故不堪大乘化

015

聲聞獨覺乘及以大乘中
不堪受化者應置於福處

016

若人不堪受天及解脫化
便以現世利如力應當攝

017

菩薩於眾生無緣能教化
當起大慈悲不應便棄捨

018

施攝及說法復聽聞說法
亦行利他事此為攝方便

019

所作益眾生不倦不放逸
起願為菩提利世即自利

繁體字

013

化恒沙众生令得罗汉果
化一入大乘此福德为上

014

教以声闻乘及独觉乘者
以彼少力故不堪大乘化

015

声闻独觉乘及以大乘中
不堪受化者应置于福处

016

若人不堪受天及解脱化
便以现世利如力应当摄

017

菩萨于众生无缘能教化
当起大慈悲不应便弃舍

018

施摄及说法复听闻说法
亦行利他事此为摄方便

019

所作益众生不倦不放逸
起愿为菩提利世即自利

简体字

013

Even if one taught beings as numerous as the Ganges' sands
So that they were caused to gain the fruit of arhatship,
Still, by instructing but a single person to enter the Great Vehicle,
One would generate merit superior to that.

014

Instructing through resort to the Śrāvaka Vehicle
Or through resort to the Pratyekabuddha Vehicle
Is undertaken where, on account of lesser abilities,
Beings are unable to accept instruction in the Great Vehicle.

015

Where even when relying on Śrāvaka or Pratyekabuddha Vehicles
In addition to the Great Vehicle teachings,
There are those who still cannot accept any such instruction,
One should strive to establish them in merit-creating situations.

016

If there be persons unable to accept
Instruction conducing either to the heavens or to liberation,
Favor them through bestowing present-life benefits.
Then, as befits one's powers, one should draw them in.

017

Where, with regard to particular beings, a bodhisattva
Has no conditions through which to instruct them,
He should draw forth the great kindness and compassion
And should refrain from abandoning them.

018

Drawing them in through giving, through explaining Dharma,
Through listening to them discuss the Dharma,
Or through endeavors beneficial to them—
These are skillful means through which to attract them.

019

In that which is done for the benefit of beings,
Do not succumb to either weariness or negligence.
Bring forth vows for the sake of realizing bodhi.
Benefiting the world is just benefiting self.

繁體字	简体字
020 入甚深法界滅離於分別 悉無有功用諸處自然捨	**020** 入甚深法界灭离于分别 悉无有功用诸处自然舍
021 利名讚樂等四處皆不著 反上亦無礙此等名為捨	**021** 利名赞乐等四处皆不着 反上亦无碍此等名为舍
022 菩薩為菩提乃至未不退 譬如燃頭衣應作是勤行	**022** 菩萨为菩提乃至未不退 譬如燃头衣应作是勤行
023 然彼諸菩薩為求菩提時 精進不應息以荷重擔故	**023** 然彼诸菩萨为求菩提时 精进不应息以荷重担故
024 未生大悲忍雖得不退轉 菩薩猶有死以起放逸故	**024** 未生大悲忍虽得不退转 菩萨犹有死以起放逸故
025 聲聞獨覺地若入便為死 以斷於菩薩諸所解知根	**025** 声闻独觉地若入便为死 以断于菩萨诸所解知根
026 假使墮泥犁菩薩不生怖 聲聞獨覺地便為大恐怖	**026** 假使堕泥犁菩萨不生怖 声闻独觉地便为大恐怖

020

Entering the extremely profound Dharma-realm,
One extinguishes mental discriminations.
As they are devoid of any useful function,
In all contexts, one naturally abides in equanimity.

021

Personal gain, reputation, praise, and happiness—
One refrains from attachment to any of these four points.
Nor do their opposites present any sort of obstacle.
This is the sort of conduct comprising equanimity.

022

So long as he has not yet gained irreversibility,
In the bodhisattva's striving for bodhi,
He should be as intensely diligent in practice
As someone whose turban has caught on fire.

023

Thus it is that those bodhisattvas,
When striving for the realization of bodhi,
Should not rest in their practice of vigor,
For they have shouldered such a heavy burden.

024

Until one develops the great compassion and the patiences,
Even though he may have gained irreversibility,
The bodhisattva is still subject to a form of "dying"
Occurring through the arising of negligence.

025

The grounds of the Śrāvakas or the Pratyekabuddhas,
If entered, constitute "death" for him
Because he would thereby sever the roots
Of the bodhisattva's understanding and awareness.

026

At the prospect of falling into the hell-realms,
The bodhisattva would not be struck with fright.
The grounds of the Śrāvakas and the Pratyekabuddhas
Do provoke great terror in him.

027

非墮泥犁中畢竟障菩提
聲聞獨覺地則為畢竟障

028

如說愛壽人怖畏於斬首
聲聞獨覺地應作如是怖

029

不生亦不滅非不生不滅
非俱不俱說空不空亦爾

030

隨何所有法於中觀不動
彼是無生忍斷諸分別故

031

既獲此忍已即時得授記
汝必當作佛便得不退轉

032

已住不動諸菩薩得於法爾
不退智
彼智二乘不能轉是故獨得
不退名

033

菩薩乃至得諸佛現前住
牢固三摩提不應起放逸

027

非墮泥犁中毕竟障菩提
声闻独觉地则为毕竟障

028

如说爱寿人怖畏于斩首
声闻独觉地应作如是怖

029

不生亦不灭非不生不灭
非俱不俱说空不空亦尔

030

随何所有法于中观不动
彼是无生忍断诸分别故

031

既获此忍已即时得授记
汝必当作佛便得不退转

032

已住不动诸菩萨得于法尔
不退智
彼智二乘不能转是故独得
不退名

033

菩萨乃至得诸佛现前住
牢固三摩提不应起放逸

繁體字   简体字

027

It is not the case that falling into the hell realms
Would create an ultimate obstacle to bodhi.
If one fell onto the grounds of the Śrāvakas or Pratyekabuddhas,
That would create an ultimate obstacle.

028

Just as is said of one who loves long life
That he is frightened at the prospect of being beheaded,
So too the grounds of the Śrāvakas and Pratyekabuddhas
Should provoke in one this very sort of fear.

029

As for "not produced and not destroyed,"
And "neither unproduced nor undestroyed,"
One denies assertions of "both" and "neither."
So too in cases involving "emptiness" and "non-emptiness."

030

No matter which "existent" dharma one encounters,
One persists therein in the contemplation, remaining unmoving.
That is the "unproduced-dharmas patience."
It is based on the severance of all mental discriminations.

031

Once one gains this patience,
One immediately receives the prediction:
"You will definitely become a buddha."
It is then that one achieves "irreversibility."

032

Those bodhisattvas already dwelling at the stage of immovability
Have gained irreversible wisdom cognizing all dharmas' reality.
As their wisdom cannot be turned back by two-vehicles adherents,
It is only at this point that they are designated as "irreversible."

033

Until the bodhisattva has gained
The solid samādhis
On the ground of all Buddhas' "direct presence,"
He should not allow any negligence to arise.

034
諸佛現前住牢固三摩提
此為菩薩父大悲忍為母

035
智度以為母方便為父者
以生及持故說菩薩父母

036
少少積聚福不能得菩提
百須彌量福聚勝乃能得

037
雖作小福德此亦有方便
於諸眾生所應悉起攀緣

038
我有諸動作常為利眾生
如是等心行誰能量其福

039
不愛自親屬及與身命財
不貪樂自在梵世及餘天

040
亦不貪涅槃為於眾生故
此唯念眾生其福誰能量

034
诸佛现前住牢固三摩提
此为菩萨父大悲忍为母

035
智度以为母方便为父者
以生及持故说菩萨父母

036
少少积聚福不能得菩提
百须弥量福聚胜乃能得

037
虽作小福德此亦有方便
于诸众生所应悉起攀缘

038
我有诸动作常为利众生
如是等心行谁能量其福

039
不爱自亲属及与身命财
不贪乐自在梵世及馀天

040
亦不贪涅盘为于众生故
此唯念众生其福谁能量

繁體字   简体字

034
The solid samādhis
On the ground of all Buddhas' "direct presence"
Serve for the bodhisattva as his father,
Whereas the great compassion and patiences serve as his mother.

035
As for the perfection of wisdom being his mother
And skillful means being his father,
It is because the one gives him birth and the other supports him
That they are said to be the bodhisattva's father and mother.

036
With but a lesser accumulation of merit
One remains unable to realize bodhi.
Only by collecting merit more massive than a hundred Sumerus
Can one succeed in achieving that realization.

037
Although one may perform but a minor meritorious deed,
Even in this, one possesses a skillful means:
Taking the sphere of "all beings" as the object,
One should generate a mental transformation of the conditions.

038
Where one reflects: "May whatever actions I undertake
Always be done for the welfare of beings,"
Who could measure the merit of he
Whose mental actions are of this sort?

039
Where one isn't constrained by fondness for relatives, retinue,
Body, life, or wealth,
Where one isn't held back by desiring pleasure in Iśvara's heavens,
Brahma-world heavens, or any other heavens,

040
Where one isn't constrained even by coveting nirvāṇa,
Where one's actions are done for the sake of other beings,
And where in all this, one thinks only of the welfare of beings,
Who then could measure the vastness of his merit?

041
無依護世間救護其苦惱
起如是心行其福誰能量

042
智度習相應如搆牛乳頃
一月復多月其福誰能量

043
佛所讚深經自誦亦教他
及為分別說是名福德聚

044
令無量眾生發心為菩提
福藏更增勝當得不動地

045
隨轉佛所轉最勝之法輪
寂滅諸惡刺是菩薩福藏

046
為利樂眾生忍地獄大苦
何況餘小苦菩提在右手

047
起作不自為唯利樂眾生
皆由大悲故菩提在右手

041
无依护世间救护其苦恼
起如是心行其福谁能量

042
智度习相应如搆牛乳顷
一月复多月其福谁能量

043
佛所赞深经自诵亦教他
及为分别说是名福德聚

044
令无量众生发心为菩提
福藏更增胜当得不动地

045
随转佛所转最胜之法轮
寂灭诸恶刺是菩萨福藏

046
为利乐众生忍地狱大苦
何况馀小苦菩提在右手

047
起作不自为唯利乐众生
皆由大悲故菩提在右手

繁體字　　　　　　　　简体字

041

When for those of the world without refuge or protection,
He rescues and protects them from their bitter afflictions—
When he raises forth such thoughts and actions as these,
Who could possibly measure his merit?

042

It would be so even in according with the perfection of wisdom
For only the moment of tugging forth a stream of cow's milk.
If one acted thus for a month or for many more months,
Who could possibly measure his merit?

043

Where one recites to himself or teaches to others
Those profound sutras praised by the Buddhas—
Also, where one interprets and explains them for others—
These are the bases of an accumulation of merit.

044

Through influencing countless beings
To generate the bodhi resolve,
One's treasury of merit increases yet more
And one becomes bound to gain "the ground of immovability."

045

Where one follows in turning what the Buddha turned,
The wheel of the supreme Dharma,
Thus clearing away all of the "noxious thorns,"
This creates the bodhisattva's treasury of merit.

046

Where, to benefit beings and make them happy,
One would endure even the sufferings of the great hells,
How much the more the other lesser sufferings,
It is as if bodhi lay in the palm of one's own right hand.

047

Where whatever one does, it is not for one's self,
But solely to benefit beings and make them happy—
Because this all arises from the great compassion,
It is as if bodhi lay in the palm of one's own right hand.

繁體字	简体字
048 智慧離戲論精進離懈怠 捨施離慳惜菩提在右手	**048** 智慧离戏论精进离懈怠 舍施离悭惜菩提在右手
049 無依無覺定圓滿無雜戒 無所從生忍菩提在右手	**049** 无依无觉定圆满无杂戒 无所从生忍菩提在右手
050 現在十方住所有諸正覺 我悉在彼前陳說我不善	**050** 现在十方住所有诸正觉 我悉在彼前陈说我不善
051 於彼十方界若佛得菩提 而不演說法我請轉法輪	**051** 于彼十方界若佛得菩提 而不演说法我请转法轮
052 現在十方界所有諸正覺 若欲捨命行頂禮勸請住	**052** 现在十方界所有诸正觉 若欲舍命行顶礼劝请住
053 若諸眾生等從於身口意 所生施戒福及以思惟修	**053** 若诸众生等从于身口意 所生施戒福及以思惟修
054 聖人及凡夫過現未來世 所有積聚福我皆生隨喜	**054** 圣人及凡夫过现未来世 所有积聚福我皆生随喜

048

Where wisdom is such that one abandons frivolous discourse,
Where vigor is such that one abandons indolence,
And where giving is such that one abandons miserliness,
It is as if bodhi lay in the palm of one's own right hand.

049

Where meditation is such that one is free of reliances or ideation,
Where morality is such that its practice is perfect and unmixed,
And where patience is such that one realizes non-production,
It is as if bodhi lay in the palm of one's own right hand.

050

In the abodes of all who have gained the right enlightenment,
Now abiding throughout the ten directions,
I appear there in the presence of them all,
And completely lay forth all my unwholesome deeds.

051

Where there are buddhas who have realized bodhi
In those realms throughout the ten directions,
But they have not yet proclaimed the Dharma,
I entreat them to turn the Dharma wheel.

052

Wherever there are those possessing the right enlightenment
Abiding in the present era in the ten directions' realms,
But now on the verge of relinquishing their lives and actions,
I bow down my head in reverence, beseeching them to remain.

053

Wherever there may be any beings
Who, by acts of body, mouth, or mind,
Have created any merit through giving, moral virtue,
And so forth, including through cultivation of meditation—

054

No matter whether they be āryas or common persons—
And no matter whether its creation is past, present, or future—
I am moved to rejoice
In all of that accumulated merit.

055

若我所有福悉以為一摶
迴與諸眾生為令得正覺

056

我如是悔過勸請隨喜福
及迴向菩提當知如諸佛

057

說悔我罪惡請佛隨喜福
及迴向菩提如最勝所說

058

右膝輪著地一髆整上衣
晝夜各三時合掌如是作

059

一時所作福若有形色者
恒沙數大千亦不能容受

060

彼初發心已於諸小菩薩
當起尊重愛猶如師父母

061

菩薩雖有過猶尚不應說
何況無實事唯應如實讚

055

若我所有福悉以为一抟
迴与诸众生为令得正觉

056

我如是悔过劝请随喜福
及迴向菩提当知如诸佛

057

说悔我罪恶请佛随喜福
及迴向菩提如最胜所说

058

右膝轮着地一髆整上衣
昼夜各三时合掌如是作

059

一时所作福若有形色者
恒沙数大千亦不能容受

060

彼初发心已于诸小菩萨
当起尊重爱犹如师父母

061

菩萨虽有过犹尚不应说
何况无实事唯应如实赞

繁體字　　　　　　　　　　　　　简体字

055

If all of the merit I have created
Could be formed into a single ball,
I would bestow it on all beings through dedicating it
To causing them to gain the right enlightenment.

056

As for these actions I undertake in repenting transgressions,
In entreating and beseeching, in rejoicing in others' merit,
And so on, including in dedicating all merit to realizing bodhi—
One should realize they accord with all buddhas' own practices.

057

These acts of confession and repentance of my bad karmic deeds,
Of entreating the Buddhas, of rejoicing in others' merit,
And so on, including dedicating all merit to realizing bodhi—
These all accord with teachings set forth by the Victorious One.

058

Kneeling down with the right knee touching the ground
And the upper robe arranged to bare one shoulder,
Three times each day and three times each night,
Press the palms together and proceed in this manner.

059

The merit created in even a single instance of doing this,
If manifest in material form, would be so immense
That even a Ganges' sands of great chiliocosms
Would still be unable to contain it.

060

Having brought forth the initial resolve,
In relations with minor bodhisattvas,
One should bring forth for them veneration and cherishing
Comparable to that felt for the Guru and parents.

061

Although a bodhisattva may have committed transgressions,
One should still not speak about them,
How much the less so where there is no truth to the matter.
One should utter praises only where they are grounded in truth.

062
若人願作佛欲使不退轉
示現及熾盛亦令生喜悅

063
未解甚深經勿言非佛說
若作如是言受最苦惡報

064
無間等諸罪悉以為一搏
比前二種罪分數不能及

065
於三解脫門應當善修習
初空次無相第三是無願

066
無自性故空已空何作相
諸相既寂滅智者何所願

067
於此修念時趣近涅槃道
勿念非佛體於彼莫放逸

068
我於涅槃中不應即作證
當發如是心應成熟智度

繁體字

062
若人愿作佛欲使不退转
示现及炽盛亦令生喜悦

063
未解甚深经勿言非佛说
若作如是言受最苦恶报

064
无间等诸罪悉以为一抟
比前二种罪分数不能及

065
于三解脱门应当善修习
初空次无相第三是无愿

066
无自性故空已空何作相
诸相既寂灭智者何所愿

067
于此修念时趣近涅盘道
勿念非佛体于彼莫放逸

068
我于涅盘中不应即作证
当发如是心应成熟智度

简体字

062

Where someone has vowed to become a buddha
And one wishes to prevent his retreat from that resolve,
Reveal the way with such clarity he brims with intense vigor,
And cause him to be filled with delight.

063

Where one hasn't yet understood extremely profound scriptures,
One must not claim they were not spoken by a buddha.
If one makes statements of this sort,
One suffers the most bitter and horrible of karmic retributions.

064

If the karmic offenses generating "non-intermittent" retributions
Were all put together to form a single ball
And were compared to one formed from the above two offenses,
They would not amount to even the smallest fraction thereof.

065

One should skillfully cultivate
The three gates to liberation:
The first is emptiness, the next is signlessness,
And the third is wishlessness.

066

Because they have no self-existent nature, phenomena are empty.
If already empty, how could one establish any characteristic signs?
Since all characteristic signs are themselves in a state of cessation,
What could there be in them that the wise might wish for?

067

When cultivating the mindful awareness of these,
One draws close to those paths leading into nirvāṇa.
Do not bear in mind anything not resulting in a buddha's body
And, in that matter, one must not allow any negligence.

068

"In this matter of nirvāṇa,
I must not immediately invoke its realization."
One should initiate this sort of resolve,
For one must succeed in ripening the perfection of wisdom.

069	069
如射師放箭各各轉相射 相持不令墮大菩薩亦爾	如射师放箭各各转相射 相持不令堕大菩萨亦尔
070	070
解脫門空中善放於心箭 巧便箭續持不令墮涅槃	解脱门空中善放于心箭 巧便箭续持不令堕涅盘
071	071
我不捨眾生為利眾生故 先起如是意次後習相應	我不舍众生为利众生故 先起如是意次后习相应
072	072
有著眾生等久夜及現行 顛倒與諸相皆以癡迷故	有着众生等久夜及现行 颠倒与诸相皆以痴迷故
073	073
著相顛倒者說法為斷除 先發如是心次後習相應	着相颠倒者说法为断除 先发如是心次后习相应
074	074
菩薩利眾生而不見眾生 此亦最難事希有不可思	菩萨利众生而不见众生 此亦最难事希有不可思
075	075
雖入正定位習應解脫門 未滿本願故不證於涅槃	虽入正定位习应解脱门 未满本愿故不证于涅盘
繁體字	简体字

069

Just as an archer might shoot his arrows upwards,
Causing each in succession to strike the one before,
Each holding up the other so none are allowed to fall—
Just so it is with the great bodhisattva.

070

Into the emptiness of the gates to liberation,
He skillfully releases the arrows of the mind.
Through artful skillful means, arrows are continuously held aloft,
So none are allowed to fall back down into nirvāṇa.

071

"I shall not forsake beings,
But rather shall continue on for the sake of benefiting beings."
One first initiates this very sort of intention,
And thenceforth ensures that his practice corresponds thereto.

072

There are beings who have become inured to attachment
Throughout time's long night and in present actions as well.
Their coursing in inverted views regarding characteristic signs
Is in every case due to confusion wrought by delusion.

073

For those attached to marks and holding inverted views,
One explains the Dharma so such errors might be eliminated.
One first generates this very sort of resolve,
And thenceforth ensures that his practice corresponds thereto.

074

The bodhisattva benefits beings
And yet does not perceive the existence of any being.
This in itself is the most difficult of all endeavors
And is such a rarity as to be inconceivable.

075

Although one may have entered "the right and definite position,"
And one's practice may accord with the gates to liberation,
Because one has not yet fulfilled one's original vows,
One refrains from proceeding to the realization of nirvāṇa.

076
若未到定位巧便力攝故
以未滿本願亦不證涅槃

077
極厭於流轉而亦向流轉
信樂於涅槃而亦背涅槃

078
應當畏煩惱不應盡煩惱
當為集眾善以遮遮煩惱

079
菩薩煩惱性不是涅槃性
非燒諸煩惱生菩提種子

080
記彼諸眾生此記有因緣
唯是佛善巧方便到彼岸

081
如空及蓮華峻崖與深坑
界不男迦柘亦如燒種子

082
諸論及工巧明術種種業
利益世間故出生建立之

繁體字

076
若未到定位巧便力摄故
以未满本愿亦不证涅盘

077
极厌于流转而亦向流转
信乐于涅盘而亦背涅盘

078
应当畏烦恼不应尽烦恼
当为集众善以遮遮烦恼

079
菩萨烦恼性不是涅盘性
非烧诸烦恼生菩提种子

080
记彼诸众生此记有因缘
唯是佛善巧方便到彼岸

081
如空及莲华峻崖与深坑
界不男迦柘亦如烧种子

082
诸论及工巧明术种种业
利益世间故出生建立之

简体字

076

Where one has not yet reached "the definite position,"
One holds himself back through the power of skillful means.
Because one has not yet fulfilled his original vows,
In this case too, he refrains from realization of nirvāṇa.

077

Though one abides in the ultimate renunciation for cyclic existence,
He nonetheless confronts cyclic existence directly.
Though one maintains faith and happiness in nirvāṇa,
He nonetheless turns his back on realization of nirvāṇa.

078

One should dread the afflictions,
But should not end the afflictions.
To gather the manifold forms of goodness, one should
Use blocking methods to fend off afflictions.

079

For the bodhisattva, afflictions accord with his nature.
He is not one who takes nirvāṇa as his very nature.
It is not the case that the burning up of the afflictions
Allows one to generate the seed of bodhi.

080

As for the predictions bestowed on those other beings,
These predictions involved specific causal circumstances.
They were solely a function of the Buddha's artfulness
In taking the perfection of skillful means "to the far shore."

081

Similes for their plight reference "empty space," "lotus flowers,"
"Precipitous cliffs," and "a deep abyss."
Their realms bar it. Analogies cite "non-virility" and *"kācamaṇi,"*
With an additional comparison made to "burnt seeds."

082

All of the treatises as well as the specialized skills,
The occult and mundane sciences, and the various trades—
Because they bring benefit to the world,
One brings them forth and establishes them.

083
隨可化眾生界趣及生中
如念即往彼願力故受生

084
於種種惡事及諂幻眾生
應用牢鎧鉀勿厭亦勿憚

085
具足勝淨意不諂亦不幻
發露諸罪惡覆藏眾善事

086
清淨身口業亦清淨意業
修諸戒學句勿令有缺減

087
安住於正念攝緣獨靜思
用念為護已*心得無障心

088
若起分別時當覺善不善
應捨諸不善多修諸善分

089
緣境心若散應當專念知
還於彼境中隨動即令住

083
随可化众生界趣及生中
如念即往彼愿力故受生

084
于种种恶事及诌幻众生
应用牢铠钾勿厌亦勿惮

085
具足胜净意不诌亦不幻
发露诸罪恶覆藏众善事

086
清净身口业亦清净意业
修诸戒学句勿令有缺减

087
安住于正念摄缘独静思
用念为护已*心得无障心

088
若起分别时当觉善不善
应舍诸不善多修诸善分

089
缘境心若散应当专念知
还于彼境中随动即令住

繁體字　　　　　　　　　　　　简体字

083

Adapting to beings amenable to instruction,
To their worlds, rebirth destinies, and birth circumstances,
As befits one's reflections, one goes directly to them,
And, through power of vows, takes birth among them.

084

In the midst of all sorts of circumstances rife with evil,
And when among beings prone to guileful flattery and deceit,
One should don one's sturdy armor.
One must not yield to either loathing or fear.

085

One equips oneself with supremely pure intentions,
Does not resort to guileful flattery or deception,
Reveals the wrongs of his karmic offenses,
And conceals his many good deeds.

086

One purifies the karma of body and mouth
And also purifies the karma of the mind.
Cultivating observance of all passages in the moral-code training.
One must not allow any omissions or diminishment in this.

087

One establishes himself in right mindfulness,
Focuses on the object condition, and stills his thought in solitude.
Having put mindfulness to use as a guard,
The mind becomes free of any obstructive thoughts.

088

When discriminating thoughts arise,
One should realize which are good and which are unwholesome,
Should forsake any which are not good,
And extensively cultivate those which are good.

089

If the mind trained on the object becomes scattered,
One should focus one's mindful awareness,
Return it to that object,
And, whenever movement occurs, immediately cause it to halt.

090

不應緩惡取而修於精進
以不能持定是故應常修

091

若登聲聞乘及以獨覺乘
唯為自利行不捨牢精進

092

何況大丈夫自度亦度人
而當不發起俱致千倍進

093

半時或別行一時行餘道
修定不應爾應緣一境界

094

於身莫有貪於命亦勿惜
縱令護此身終是爛壞法

095

利養恭敬名一向勿貪著
當如然頭衣勤行成所願

096

決即起勝利不可待明日
明日太賒遠何緣保瞬命

繁體字

090

不应缓恶取而修于精进
以不能持定是故应常修

091

若登声闻乘及以独觉乘
唯为自利行不舍牢精进

092

何况大丈夫自度亦度人
而当不发起俱致千倍进

093

半时或别行一时行馀道
修定不应尔应缘一境界

094

于身莫有贪于命亦勿惜
纵令护此身终是烂坏法

095

利养恭敬名一向勿贪着
当如然头衣勤行成所愿

096

决即起胜利不可待明日
明日太赊远何缘保瞬命

简体字

090

One should refrain from laxity and from wrong attachment
Cultivated with intensity,
For they make it impossible to maintain concentration.
One should therefore remain constant in right cultivation.

091

Even were one to take up the vehicle of the Śrāvakas
Or the vehicle of the Pratyekabuddhas,
And hence practice solely for one's own benefit,
One would still not relinquish the enduring practice of vigor.

092

How much the less could it be that a great man
Committed to liberate both himself and all others
Might somehow fail to generate
A measure of vigor a thousand *koṭīs* times greater?

093

As for cultivating some other practice half the time
Or simultaneously practicing some other path,
One should not do this when cultivating meditative concentration.
One should rather focus exclusively on a single objective condition.

094

One must not indulge any covetousness regarding the body
And must not cherish even one's own life.
Even were one to allow any protectiveness toward this body,
It is but a dharma bound in the end to rot away.

095

One must never develop a covetous attachment
To offerings, reverence from others, or fame.
Rather one should strive diligently to fulfill one's vows,
Acting with the urgency of one whose turban has caught fire.

096

Acting resolutely and immediately, pull forth the supreme benefit.
In this, one cannot wait for tomorrow.
Tomorrow is too distant a time,
For how can one ensure survival even for the blink of an eye?

097

安住於正命如食愛子肉
於所食噉中勿愛亦勿嫌

098

出家為何義我所作竟未
今思為作不如十法經說

099

觀有為無常若無我我所
所有諸魔業應覺而捨離

100

根力與覺分神足正斷道
及以四念處為修發精勤

101

心與利樂善作傳傳生處
及諸惡濁根彼當善觀察

102

我於善法中日日何增長
復有何損減彼應極觀察

103

見他得增長利養恭敬名
微小慳嫉心皆所不應作

繁體字

097

安住于正命如食爱子肉
于所食噉中勿爱亦勿嫌

098

出家为何义我所作竟未
今思为作不如十法经说

099

观有为无常若无我我所
所有诸魔业应觉而舍离

100

根力与觉分神足正断道
及以四念处为修发精勤

101

心与利乐善作传传生处
及诸恶浊根彼当善观察

102

我于善法中日日何增长
复有何损减彼应极观察

103

见他得增长利养恭敬名
微小悭嫉心皆所不应作

简体字

097

Having established oneself in right livelihood,
When eating, it is as if consuming the flesh of a cherished son.
One must not indulge in either affection for or disapproval of
Whatever food one has taken for the meal.

098

For what purpose has one left the home life?
Have I finished what is to be done or not?
Reflect now on whether or not one is doing the work,
Doing so as described in the Ten Dharmas Sutra.

099

Contemplate conditioned phenomena as impermanent,
As devoid of self, and as devoid of anything belonging to a self.
One must become aware of and withdraw from
All forms of demonic karmic activity.

100

Generate energetic diligence in order to cultivate
The roots, powers, limbs of enlightenment,
Bases of spiritual powers, right severances, the Path,
And the four stations of mindfulness.

101

The mind may serve as a source for the repeated generation
Of good deeds bestowing benefit and happiness
Or it may instead serve as the root of all sorts of evil and turbidity.
One should make it the focus of skillful analytic contemplation.

102

"From one day to the next, what increase has occurred
In my cultivation of good dharmas?"
"Also, what diminishment has occurred in this?"
Those should be the contemplations of utmost concern.

103

Whenever one observes someone else experiencing an increase
In offerings, reverences, or reputation,
Even the most subtle thoughts of stinginess and jealously
Should never be indulged.

104

不羨諸境界行癡盲瘂聾
時復師子吼怖諸外道鹿

105

奉迎及將送應敬所尊重
於諸法事中隨順而佐助

106

救脫被殺者自然增不減
善修明巧業自學亦教他

107

於諸勝善法牢固而受之
修行四攝事施衣及飲食

108

不違乞求者和合諸親戚
眷屬不乖離施宅及財物

109

父母及親友隨所應安置
所應安置處無上自在主

110

雖復是奴僕善說亦受取
應生最尊重施藥愈諸病

104

不羡诸境界行痴盲瘂聋
时复师子吼怖诸外道鹿

105

奉迎及将送应敬所尊重
于诸法事中随顺而佐助

106

救脱被杀者自然增不减
善修明巧业自学亦教他

107

于诸胜善法牢固而受之
修行四摄事施衣及饮食

108

不违乞求者和合诸亲戚
眷属不乖离施宅及财物

109

父母及亲友随所应安置
所应安置处无上自在主

110

虽复是奴仆善说亦受取
应生最尊重施药愈诸病

繁體字　　　　　　　　　　　　　简体字

104

One should not cherish any aspect of the objective realms,
But rather should act as if dull-witted, blind, mute, and deaf.
Still, when timely, respond by roaring the lion's roar,
Frightening off the non-Buddhist deer.

105

In welcoming them on arrival and escorting them off as they go,
One should be reverential toward those worthy of veneration.
In all endeavors associated with the Dharma,
One should follow along, participate, and contribute assistance.

106

One rescues and liberates beings bound to be killed.
One's goodness increases and never decreases.
One well cultivates karmic works involving the sciences and skills,
Training in them oneself while also teaching them to others.

107

Adopt all of the supremely good dharmas,
Through persistent and solid practice.
Cultivate the four means of attraction,
Making gifts of robes and food and drink.

108

Do not turn away from those begging for alms.
Facilitate the uniting of close relatives.
Prevent estrangement between those of the same clan.
Make gifts of dwellings and of material possessions as well.

109

As for one's father, mother, relatives, and friends,
Provide them circumstances befitting their station.
Wherever one has given them such a suitable situation,
Treat them as supreme and independent sovereigns.

110

Although there may be yet others who are servants,
One speaks to them with goodness and, in effect, adopts them.
One should accord them the highest esteem
And provide them with medicines and treatment for all illnesses.

111

前行善業首細滑美妙言
善為正意語前後無不供

112

不壞他眷屬慈眼觀眾生
亦不以嫌心皆如善親友

113

應當如所言即隨如是作
如言若即作他人則生信

114

應當擁護法覺察放逸者
及作金寶網羅覆於支提

115

有欲求婇女莊嚴以施之
亦與說佛德及施雜光瓔

116

造作佛形像端坐勝蓮花
及於六法中修習同喜樂

117

可供無不供為命亦不謗
佛之所說法及以說法人

繁體字

111

前行善业首细滑美妙言
善为正意语前后无不供

112

不坏他眷属慈眼观众生
亦不以嫌心皆如善亲友

113

应当如所言即随如是作
如言若即作他人则生信

114

应当拥护法觉察放逸者
及作金宝网罗覆于支提

115

有欲求婇女庄严以施之
亦与说佛德及施杂光璎

116

造作佛形像端坐胜莲花
及于六法中修习同喜乐

117

可供无不供为命亦不谤
佛之所说法及以说法人

简体字

111

Be the first to act, taking the lead in good karmic deeds,
Speaking with smooth and sublime words,
Being skillful in discourse guided by right intention,
And having no one above or below to whom gifts are not given.

112

Avoid any harm to the retinue of others.
Instead regard beings with the eye of kindness.
Neither may one course in disapproving thoughts.
Instead treat everyone as a good relative or friend.

113

One should accord with the words he speaks,
Following them straightaway with concordant actions.
If one acts immediately in accordance with his words,
Others will be inclined then to develop faith.

114

One should support and protect the Dharma,
And should discover any instances of neglect,
Even going so far as to build canopies graced by gold and jewels
Spreading over and covering the *caityas*.

115

For those wishing to obtain a maiden mate,
See to her adornment and assist in her presentation.
Speak to the parties about the qualities of the Buddha
And then give prayer beads gleaming in varying hues.

116

Create images of the Buddha
Sitting upright atop supremely fine lotus blossoms
And cultivate common delight and happiness
Through adherence to the six dharmas of community harmony.

117

Of those who may be given offerings, none are not given offerings.
Even for the sake of preserving one's life, one still does not slander
The Dharma spoken by the Buddha
Or the person who expounds the Dharma.

繁體字	简体字
118 金寶散教師及教師支提 若有忘所誦與念令不失	**118** 金宝散教师及教师支提 若有忘所诵与念令不失
119 未思所作已勿躁勿隨他 外道天龍神於中皆莫信	**119** 未思所作已勿躁勿随他 外道天龙神于中皆莫信
120 心應如金剛堪能通諸法 心亦應如山諸事所不動	**120** 心应如金刚堪能通诸法 心亦应如山诸事所不动
121 憙樂出世語莫樂依世言 自受諸功德亦應令他受	**121** 憙乐出世语莫乐依世言 自受诸功德亦应令他受
122 修五解脫入修十不淨想 八大丈夫覺亦應分別修	**122** 修五解脱入修十不净想 八大丈夫觉亦应分别修
123 天耳與天眼神足與他心 及與宿命住應修淨五通	**123** 天耳与天眼神足与他心 及与宿命住应修净五通
124 四神足為根欲進心思惟 四無量住持謂慈悲喜捨	**124** 四神足为根欲进心思惟 四无量住持谓慈悲喜舍

118

Gold and jewels are distributed among teaching masters
And also among the *caityas* of teaching masters.
If there are those who forget what is to be recited,
One assists their remembrance, enabling them to stay free of error.

119

When one has not yet reflected on the right course of action,
One must not be impulsive and must not simply emulate others.
As for the non-Buddhists, gods, dragons, and spirits,
One must not invest one's faith in any of them.

120

One's mind should be like *vajra*,
Able to penetrate all dharmas.
One's mind should also be like a mountain,
Remaining unmoved in any circumstance.

121

Delight in world-transcending discourse
And do not take pleasure in worldly words.
Personally adopt all manner of meritorious qualities.
One should then influence others to adopt them as well.

122

Cultivate the five bases of liberation.
Cultivate the ten reflections on impurity.
The eight realizations of great men
Should also be the focus of analytic contemplation and cultivation.

123

The heavenly ear, the heavenly eye,
The bases of spiritual powers, the cognition of others' thoughts,
And the cognition of past lives and abodes—
One should cultivate purification of these five spiritual abilities.

124

The four bases of spiritual powers comprise their root.
They are zeal, vigor, mental focus, and contemplative reflection.
The four immeasurables govern them.
They are kindness, compassion, sympathetic joy, and equanimity.

125

四界如毒蛇六入如空村
五眾如殺者應作如是觀

126

重法及法師亦捨於法慳
教師勿捲祕聽者勿散亂

127

無慢無希望唯以悲愍心
尊重恭敬意為眾而說法

128

於聞無厭足聞已皆誦持
不誑尊福田亦令師歡喜

129

不應觀他家心懷於敬養
勿以論難故習誦於世典

130

勿以瞋恚故毀呰諸菩薩
未受未聞法亦勿生誹謗

131

斷除於憍慢當住四聖種
勿嫌於他人亦勿自高舉

繁體字

125

四界如毒蛇六入如空村
五众如杀者应作如是观

126

重法及法师亦舍于法悭
教师勿卷秘听者勿散乱

127

无慢无希望唯以悲愍心
尊重恭敬意为众而说法

128

于闻无厌足闻已皆诵持
不诳尊福田亦令师欢喜

129

不应观他家心怀于敬养
勿以论难故习诵于世典

130

勿以瞋恚故毁呰诸菩萨
未受未闻法亦勿生诽谤

131

断除于憍慢当住四圣种
勿嫌于他人亦勿自高举

简体字

125

The four elements are like poisonous serpents.
The six sense faculties are like an empty village.
The five aggregates are like assassins.
One should contemplate them in this way.

126

Esteem the Dharma and the masters of Dharma
And also relinquish any stinginess with the Dharma.
The instructing masters must not be tight-fisted or secretive
And those listening must not be mentally scattered or confused.

127

Free of arrogance and free of hopes,
Motivated solely by thoughts of compassion and pity,
With reverent and respectful mind,
Expound the Dharma for the community.

128

Be insatiable in learning
And always recite and retain what has been learned.
Do not deceive any among the venerable fields of merit.
Moreover, cause one's instructors to be delighted.

129

One should not pay visits to the houses of others
With a mind cherishing reverence or offerings.
One must not take up study and recitation of worldly texts
For the sake of debating challenging topics.

130

One must not be provoked by hatefulness or anger
Into defaming any bodhisattva.
As for dharmas not yet received or learned,
One must not initiate slanders in those cases either.

131

In order to cut off arrogance and pride,
One should abide in the four lineage bases of the ārya.
One must not course in disapproval of others
And must not allow oneself to become conceited.

132

若實不實犯不得發覺他
勿求他錯失自錯當覺知

133

佛及諸佛法不應分別疑
法雖最難信於中應信之

134

雖由實語死退失轉輪王
及以諸天王唯應作實語

135

打罵恐殺縛終不怨責他
皆是我自罪業報故來現

136

應極尊重愛供養於父母
亦給侍和上恭敬阿闍梨

137

為信聲聞乘及以獨覺乘
說於最深法此是菩薩錯

138

為信深大乘眾生而演說
聲聞獨覺乘此亦是其錯

132

若实不实犯不得发觉他
勿求他错失自错当觉知

133

佛及诸佛法不应分别疑
法虽最难信于中应信之

134

虽由实语死退失转轮王
及以诸天王唯应作实语

135

打骂恐杀缚终不怨责他
皆是我自罪业报故来现

136

应极尊重爱供养于父母
亦给侍和上恭敬阿闍梨

137

为信声闻乘及以独觉乘
说于最深法此是菩萨错

138

为信深大乘众生而演说
声闻独觉乘此亦是其错

繁體字   简体字

132

Whether or not someone has actually committed a transgression,
One must not reveal his situation to others.
Do not seek out the errors and faults of anyone else.
Rather one should become aware of one's own errors.

133

One should refrain from biased judgments and doubting
In fathoming the Buddha and the Dharma of the Buddhas.
Even though a dharma may be extremely difficult to believe,
One should nonetheless maintain faith in it.

134

Even though one might be put to death for speaking the truth,
Or might be forced to abdicate the throne of a universal monarch,
Or even that of a king among the gods,
One should still utter only truthful speech.

135

Even if beaten, cursed, or terrorized with death threats or captivity,
One must not hate or condemn others, but should instead reflect:
"This is all the product of my own karmic offenses.
This has happened as a result of karmic retribution."

136

One should, with the most ultimate respect and affection,
Provide offerings in support of one's father and mother.
Also supply the needs of and serve the *upādhyāyas*,
While extending reverence to the *ācāryas* as well.

137

When, for those who place their faith in the Śrāvaka Vehicle
Or those dedicated to the Pratyekabuddha Vehicle,
One discourses on the most profound of dharmas,
This, for a bodhisattva, is an error.

138

When, for believers in the profound Great-Vehicle teachings,
One discourses to those beings
On the Śrāvaka or Pratyekabuddha vehicles,
This too is an error for him.

139
大人來求法慢緩不為說
而反攝受惡委任無信者

140
遠捨所說錯所說頭多德
於彼當念知亦皆應習近

141
等心平等說平等善安立
亦令正相應諸眾生無別

142
為法不為利為德不為名
欲脫眾生苦不欲自身樂

143
密意求業果所作福事生
亦為成熟眾捨離於自事

144
親近善知識所謂法師佛
勸勵出家者及以乞求輩

145
依止世論者專求世財者
信解獨覺乘及以聲聞乘

繁體字

139
大人来求法慢缓不为说
而反摄受恶委任无信者

140
远舍所说错所说头多德
于彼当念知亦皆应习近

141
等心平等说平等善安立
亦令正相应诸众生无别

142
为法不为利为德不为名
欲脱众生苦不欲自身乐

143
密意求业果所作福事生
亦为成熟众舍离于自事

144
亲近善知识所谓法师佛
劝励出家者及以乞求辈

145
依止世论者专求世财者
信解独觉乘及以声闻乘

简体字

139

So too where some superior person comes seeking the Dharma,
But one delays and fails to provide him with teachings.
So too where, on the contrary, one takes in wrongdoers
Or delegates responsibilities to those who are untrustworthy.

140

One must abandon the errors mentioned above.
As for such herein-described meritorious practices as the *dhūtas*,
One ought to become knowledgeable about them
And then incorporate them into one's own practice.

141

Regard all equally in one's thoughts, speak equally for all,
Be uniformly equal in establishing all others in goodness,
And influence them all equally to accord with what is right.
Thus one refrains from making distinctions between any beings.

142

One works for the sake of Dharma and not for self-benefit.
One works to develop meritorious qualities, not for renown.
One wishes to liberate beings from suffering
And does not wish merely to ensure his own happiness.

143

With purposes kept secret, one seeks fruition in one's works.
When the results of one's merit-generating endeavors come forth,
Even then, one applies them to the ripening of the many
While abandoning preoccupation with one's own concerns.

144

Grow close to good spiritual friends,
Specifically, to the masters of Dharma, to the Buddhas,
To those who encourage one to leave the home life,
And to those who are seekers of alms.

145

Those who ground themselves in worldly treatises,
Those who exclusively seek worldly wealth,
Those with Pratyekabuddha Vehicle faith and understanding,
And those devoted to the Śrāvaka Vehicle—

繁體字	简体字
146 此四惡知識菩薩應當知 復有應求者所謂四大藏	**146** 此四恶知识菩萨应当知 复有应求者所谓四大藏
147 佛出聞諸度及於法師所 見之心無礙樂住空閑處	**147** 佛出闻诸度及于法师所 见之心无碍乐住空闲处
148 地水火風空悉與其相似 一切處平等利益諸眾生	**148** 地水火风空悉与其相似 一切处平等利益诸众生
149 當善思惟義勤生陀羅尼 勿於聽法者為作於障礙	**149** 当善思惟义勤生陀罗尼 勿于听法者为作于障碍
150 惱中能調伏小事捨無餘 八種懈怠事皆亦應除斷	**150** 恼中能调伏小事舍无馀 八种懈怠事皆亦应除断
151 莫作非分貪橫貪不稱意 離者皆令合無問親非親	**151** 莫作非分贪横贪不称意 离者皆令合无问亲非亲
152 於空而得空智者莫依行 若當得於空彼惡過身見	**152** 于空而得空智者莫依行 若当得于空彼恶过身见

繁體字   简体字

146

As for these four types of unwholesome spiritual friends,
The bodhisattva should be aware of them as such.
There are, however, other circumstances one should seek out.
This refers specifically to the four great treasuries:

147

The emergence of buddhas; hearing the perfections explained;
Being able in the presence of a master of Dharma
To behold him with unobstructed mind;
And happily pursuing cultivation in a place of solitude.

148

Abide in a manner comparable to
Earth, water, fire, wind, and space,
Remaining thus uniformly equal under all circumstances
In providing benefit to all beings.

149

One should skillfully reflect upon the meanings
And diligently progress in the uses of the *dhāraṇīs*.
One must never create any sort of obstruction
To those seeking to hear the Dharma.

150

When embroiled in the afflictions, be able to overcome them.
Relinquish the lesser instances, retaining not a trace.
Regarding the eight cases involving indolence,
One should cut all of those off as well.

151

Do not covet what is not one's lot,
For unprincipled covetousness will not bring satisfaction.
Influence all who have become estranged to reconcile,
Whether or not they are one's own relations.

152

The wise must not base their practice
On getting at the "emptiness" in what is intrinsically empty.
In the case of one determined to get at that emptiness itself,
That wrong is even more extreme than viewing the body as a self.

153

掃塗與莊嚴及多種鼓樂
香鬘等供具供養於支提

154

作種種燈輪供養支提舍
施蓋及革屣騎乘車輿等

155

專應喜樂(去)[法]樂知信佛得
喜樂給侍僧亦樂聞正法

156

前世中不生現在中不住
後際中不到如是觀諸法

157

好事與眾生不求彼好報
當為獨忍苦不自偏受樂

158

雖足大福報心不舉不喜
雖貧如餓鬼亦不下不憂

159

若有已學者應極尊重之
未學令入學不應生輕蔑

153

扫涂与庄严及多种鼓乐
香鬘等供具供养于支提

154

作种种灯轮供养支提舍
施盖及革屣骑乘车舆等

155

专应喜乐(去)[法]乐知信佛得
喜乐给侍僧亦乐闻正法

156

前世中不生现在中不住
后际中不到如是观诸法

157

好事与众生不求彼好报
当为独忍苦不自偏受乐

158

虽足大福报心不举不喜
虽贫如饿鬼亦不下不忧

159

若有已学者应极尊重之
未学令入学不应生轻蔑

繁體字   简体字

153

By sweeping and finishing floors, by providing adornments,
By furnishing many varieties of drums and music,
And by offering fragrances, flower garlands, and other gifts,
Contribute offerings to the *caityas*.

154

Create all sorts of lantern wheels
As offerings to the *caityas* and their buildings.
Provide canopies as well as sandals,
Horse-drawn carriages, sedan chairs, and the like.

155

One should especially find delight in the Dharma
And be happy knowing what is gained through faith in Buddha.
Delight in providing for and serving the monastic Sangha,
While also finding happiness through listening to right Dharma.

156

They do not arise in the past.
They do not abide in the present.
They do not go forward into the future.
Contemplate all dharmas in this manner.

157

Give to beings whatsoever is fine
And do not wish that they bestow anything fine in return.
One should prefer it be solely oneself who endures suffering
While not favoring oneself in the enjoyment of happiness.

158

Although replete with karmic rewards from immense merit,
The mind should not become lofty or overwhelmed with delight.
Although one may be as poverty-stricken as a hungry ghost,
One should still not become downcast or overcome with distress.

159

Accord the most ultimate degree of esteem
To those already accomplished in learning.
Inspire those as yet unlearned to devote themselves to study.
One should not behave in a manner belittling them.

160

戒具者恭敬破戒令入戒
智具者親近愚者令住智

161

流轉苦多種生老死惡趣
不怖此等畏當降魔惡智

162

所有諸佛土摶聚諸功德
為皆得彼故發願及精進

163

恒於諸法中不取而行捨
此為諸眾生受擔欲荷負

164

正觀於諸法無我無我所
亦勿捨大悲及以於大慈

165

勝過諸供養以供佛世尊
彼作何者是所謂法供養

166

若持菩薩藏及得陀羅尼
入深法源底是為法供養

繁體字

160

戒具者恭敬破戒令入戒
智具者亲近愚者令住智

161

流转苦多种生老死恶趣
不怖此等畏当降魔恶智

162

所有诸佛土抟聚诸功德
为皆得彼故发愿及精进

163

恒于诸法中不取而行舍
此为诸众生受担欲荷负

164

正观于诸法无我无我所
亦勿舍大悲及以于大慈

165

胜过诸供养以供佛世尊
彼作何者是所谓法供养

166

若持菩萨藏及得陀罗尼
入深法源底是为法供养

简体字

160

Revere those perfect in observance of the moral precepts
And influence those who break precepts to take on the precepts.
Draw close to those perfect in wisdom
And influence those who act foolishly to abide in wisdom.

161

The sufferings of cyclic existence are of many kinds,
Involving birth, aging, death, and the wretched destinies.
One should not be frightened by the fearsomeness of these.
One must instead subdue demons and knowledge rooted in evil.

162

Amass every form of merit
In the lands of all the Buddhas.
Bring forth vows and proceed with vigor
So that everyone may succeed in reaching them.

163

Even in the midst of all dharmas, one is constant
In not seizing on them, thus coursing along in equanimity.
One takes on the burden, wishing to bear it on forth,
Proceeding in this manner for the sake of all beings.

164

Abide in the right contemplation of all dharmas
As devoid of self and as devoid of anything belonging to a self.
Even so, one must not relinquish the great compassion
Or one's reliance on the great kindness.

165

As for that which is superior even to using every sort of gift
In making offerings to the Buddha, the Bhagavān,
What sort of action might that be?
This refers specifically to making offerings of Dharma.

166

If one preserves the Bodhisattva Canon,
Even to the point of gaining realization of the *dhāraṇīs*—
If one enters into and reaches the bottom of Dharma's source—
This is what constitutes the offering of Dharma.

167

應當依於義莫唯愛雜味

於深法道中善入莫放逸

168

如是此資糧恒沙等大劫

出家及在家當得滿正覺

167

应当依于义莫唯爱杂味

于深法道中善入莫放逸

168

如是此资粮恒沙等大劫

出家及在家当得满正觉

繁體字

简体字

167

One should rely upon the meaning.
One must not cherish only the various flavors.
In the Path of the profound Dharma
One enters with skill and must not fall prey to negligence.

168

One cultivates these provisions in this manner
For kalpas as numerous as the Ganges' sands,
Doing so sometimes as a monastic, sometimes as a householder.
Thus one will succeed in perfecting the right enlightenment.

PART TWO:

A Selective Abridgement of
THE BODHISAṂBHĀRA ŚĀSTRA COMMENTARY

Composed by the Early Indian Bhikshu Vaśitva
(circa 300–500 CE?)

With Explanatory Notes by the Translator

A Selective Abridgement of
THE BODHISAMBHĀRA ŚĀSTRA COMMENTARY

A Detailed Summary of Bhikshu Vaśitva's Commentary on
Ārya Nāgārjuna's *Bodhisambhāra Śāstra*

---

001 – The Homage to All Buddhas and the Declaration of Intent

Now, in the presence of all the Buddhas,
With palms pressed together, I bow down my head in reverence.
I shall explain here in accordance with the teachings
The provisions essential for the bodhi of the Buddhas.

AV "In the presence of all the Buddhas" refers to all Buddhas of the past, present, and future.

"Buddha" refers specifically to those who have awakened from the sleep of ignorance. This does not however include arhats, pratyekabuddhas, or bodhisattvas, this on account of the dharmas exclusive to buddhas which not even these classes of very advanced practitioners possess.

"In accordance with the teachings" indicates this has already been explained in all sorts of ways in the sutras and that now, too, this shall be explained in accordance with those teachings.

"Bodhi" is the term employed to reference the wisdom of all-knowledge.

"Provisions" is a reference to: that which preserves, that which raises and nurtures, that which forms the causal basis for bodhi, and that which represents the complete adequacy of the essential component parts of bodhi.

TN On the most elementary level, one may think of "provisions" simply as the prerequisite conditions essential to the realization of the highest enlightenment. In brief, there are two provisions to which all other provisions are reducible, namely merit and wisdom. In the absence of complete repletion in merit and wisdom, realization of buddhahood is impossible.

002 – The Impossibility of Completely Describing the Provisions

How would one be able to describe without omission
All of the provisions for the realization of bodhi?
This could only be accomplished by the Buddhas themselves,
For they, exclusively, have realized the boundless enlightenment.

AV "Boundless enlightenment" is a reference to a buddha's unimpeded knowledge of all of the boundlessly-many meanings that
need be known (for a buddha to do the work of the buddha). The
buddha's awakening transcends the "bounds" imposed by such
views as those clinging to sense pleasures or useless varieties of
asceticism, to annihilationism or eternalism, or to existence as
inherently real or unreal.

003 – Since a Buddha's Qualities are Boundless, So Too Are the Provisions

The boundless meritorious qualities of a buddha's body
Are rooted in the provisions essential to enlightenment.
Therefore the provisions for enlightenment
Themselves have no bounds.

AV There are multiple connotations of the term "meritorious qualities" as it is used here. These include:

1) Praiseworthiness.
2) Repeated involvement in the meritorious action at the root of
   the quality.
3) Durability associated with sound bases underlying the creation of the qualities.
4) Dependence upon noble bases such as the six perfections.

In the body of a buddha, these meritorious qualities are "boundless." Since they are boundless, the provisions causing them must
be boundless as well.

As for provisions being "rooted in the provisions essential to
enlightenment," this is because the provisions involved in the
acquisition of bodhi comprise the very root of the boundlessly
many meritorious qualities associated with a buddha's body.

It is especially on account of the fact that the body of a buddha
is possessed of boundlessly many meritorious qualities that it is
essential to employ the development of boundlessly many meritorious qualities in perfecting that buddha body [for one's own future

buddhahood]. Thus it is that the provisions themselves have no delimiting boundaries at all.

TN Implicit in Nāgārjuna's raising of the topic of "the boundless meritorious qualities of a buddha's body" is a reference to a buddha body's thirty-two marks and eighty subsidiary characteristics These physical characteristics are collectively emblematic of the vast range of previous-life causal practices perfected by a buddha. They are also representative of any buddha's present-moment possession of the fully-developed qualities linked to the six perfections.

The term "boundless" may seem counter-intuitive in describing what we would ordinarily think of as visually finite physical features. But the physical features of a buddha are not even delimited by visual finitude, at least when they are observed with the fully developed five spiritual eyes. Take for instance the infinitely-extending "summit" mark issuing from a buddha's crown. Even resorting to all his skills as the foremost among the Buddha's disciples in psychic power, Mahāmaudgalyāyana was still unable to find the end of its upward extension.

Another example is found in Ānanda's observation of the Buddha's "sunrise samādhi" which he was only able to perceive through the Buddha's "lending" him psychic powers he had not yet developed on his own. Ānanda discovered that the Buddha is constantly issuing transformation bodies from all of the pores of his body. Such "boundlessness," both in terms of antecedent practices and in terms of miraculous manifestations is characteristic of other physical features of a buddha's body as well.

---

004 – Reverence to Buddhas and to Bodhisattvas, Those Also Worthy of Offerings

I shall then explain but a lesser portion of them.
I render reverence to the Buddhas and the Bodhisattvas.
It is all such bodhisattvas as these
To whom one should next make offerings, after the Buddhas.

AV As for "explaining but a lesser portion," because the provisions are boundless and one's wisdom is limited, one can describe them only incompletely.

As for rendering reverence to bodhisattvas, there are seven levels of bodhisattvas:

1) Those who have generated the initial resolve.

2) Those who have taken up right cultivation.
3) Those realizing the unproduced-dharmas patience.
4) Those at the level of "anointing of the crown."
5) Those abiding at the level of "one remaining life."
6) Those at the level of their very last birth;
7) Those who have approached the site of enlightenment.

All of these bodhisattvas are worthy of reverence and offerings next in sequence after the Buddhas. This is because even the initial-resolve bodhisattva possesses the profound mind, vast in its scope, by which he embodies the capacity to completely implement the teachings of the Buddhas. All buddhas emerge from among just such bodhisattvas. This ability to carry on the lineage of the Buddhas makes such bodhisattvas superior in their capacities to all other disciples of the Buddha.

These bodhisattvas desire to influence all beings to achieve the cessation of all sufferings. It is not the case that they are motivated by the desire to bring but a lesser fraction of beings to enlightenment. Because this profound mind is so vast in the scope of its greatness, all beings should in every case be moved to offer them reverential respect.

---

005 – The Primary Provision: Prajñāpāramitā, Mother of Buddhas and Bodhisattvas

Since it is the mother of the Bodhisattvas,
It is also the mother of the Buddhas:
The prajñāpāramitā
Is the foremost among the provisions for enlightenment.

AV "It is because the perfection of prajñā is the mother of all bodhisattvas that it is foremost among the provisions for the acquisition of bodhi."

The perfection of prajñā is foremost among the provisions in just the same way as the eye faculty is most supreme among the body's sense faculties and the head is most supreme among the main parts of the body. Among all of the perfections, the perfection of prajñā is supreme.

The perfection of prajñā is "foremost" in the sense that it is the primary priority in correct practice of the other provisions. Its essentiality here is comparable to the primary role of faith in the larger sphere of all Buddhist practice. For example, giving cannot qualify as "the perfection of giving" without the presence of prajñā.

So too with the other perfections. The supremacy of the perfection of wisdom is also based on the greatness of the fruits it engenders.

The perfection of wisdom is said to be "the mother of the bodhisattvas" because it has the ability to give birth to them. It is this prajñā wisdom mediated by skillful means which brings about the birth of the bodhisattva, causing him to seek the unsurpassed bodhi of a buddha over the lesser-scope enlightenment of the Śrāvaka-disciples and the Pratyekabuddhas. It is through its causing the birth of a buddha body that the perfection of wisdom qualifies as "the mother of the Bodhisattvas."

It is also because of its inherent placement within the correct practice of the other five perfections, because of its similarity to maternally-generated assessments for the benefit of a child, because of its involvement in the decision making necessary to the maturing of a bodhisattva, and because of its path-generating abilities activated in recitation of sutras that the perfection of wisdom is said to be "the mother of the Bodhisattvas."

It is because the perfection of prajñā gives birth to and reveals unimpeded wisdom and because all buddhas are reliant upon unimpeded wisdom to extinguish the afflictions that the prajñāpāramitā is therefore also known as the mother of the Buddhas.

The prajñāpāramitā is known as such because it lies even beyond the sphere of the Śrāvaka disciples and the Pratyekabuddhas, because there is nothing beyond it worth knowing, because it enables perfection in all things, because nothing anywhere is capable of vanquishing it, and because it is uniformly equal in its manifestations throughout time and space. These causal bases are as set forth in the *Prajñāpāramitā Sutra*.

---

006 – Prajñā Includes the Remaining Five Perfections and Their Retinue

Because giving, moral virtue, patience, vigor, meditation,
And the others following from these five
All arise from the perfection of wisdom,
They are included within the pāramitās.

TN Bhikshu Vaśitva's commentary recommends that one understand "the others following from these five" as referring to the four additional perfections (skillful means, vows, powers, and knowledges). When these nine are added to their source (*prajñā*), this produces the "ten perfections" found in the Mahāyāna canon.

In his full-length commentary, Bhikshu Vaśitva now departs on a detailed tour of each of these "ten perfections." I've condensed those explanations and included them below so as to make them more readily accessible to the reader.

For a complete discussion of the perfections which demonstrates a refinement and brilliance beyond even Bhikshu Vaśitva's extended discussion, see my translation under separate cover: *Nāgārjuna on the Six Perfections*, a complete translation of sixteen consecutive chapters on this topic from Nāgārjuna's *Exegesis on the Great Perfection of Wisdom Sutra*.

Condensed Bhikshu Vaśitva Discussion of the Six Perfections
The Discussion of the Perfection of Giving

Sequencing Rationale and Valid Intended Effects of Giving

AV We treat the perfection of giving herein as the second of the bodhi provisions because prajñā is the primary priority in practice and because the bodhisattva practices giving to enable acquisition of bodhi.

Through this practice, one facilitates both physical and mental happiness in other beings. It is not that one gives to visit yet more suffering on other beings.

Categories of Giving

Giving is of two basic kinds: the giving of material wealth and the giving of Dharma. Material wealth is itself of two types: sentient and insentient.

Sentient giving is in turn of two types, personal and extrapersonal. Giving of one's limbs or entire body is "personal" whereas giving up of one's sons, daughters, wives, consorts, or other beings is "extrapersonal."

Insentient giving is of two types, consumable and nonconsumable, with anything taken internally as food or drink being the former, and most everything else being the latter.

Now, useful Dharma giving is itself of two kinds, mundane and supramundane, the former being that leading to favorable rebirth, the latter leading to transcendence of cyclic existence.

The giving of material wealth and the giving of Dharma each involve two subtypes: "involving attachment" and "free of attachment," the former being that done for one's own worldly priorities and the latter being that done either to benefit all beings or to facilitate acquisition of unimpeded wisdom.

Additional sorts of giving include "the giving of fearlessness" and other types subsumed under "the giving of material wealth." The karmic rewards and secondary effects of those two types of giving (material wealth and Dharma) are comprehensively explained in the Great Vehicle scriptures.

Bhikshu Vaśitva's Stanzas on Giving

Bhikshu Vaśitva then presents a dozen stanzas describing the giving of material wealth, personal and extrapersonal giving, giving of that which is and is not sentient, and the giving of fearlessness. Those stanzas conclude with stanzas focusing on right motivation and giving as done by bodhisattvas. He finishes those stanzas with three implicit points:

1)   When giving, reflect on recipients as "fields of merit," and as "belonging to one's own retinue of those who are good."
2)   When giving, one dedicates the karmic rewards to the pureland rebirth and future buddhahood of self and others.
3)   It is the bodhisattva's giving which is dedicated to acquisition of the body of a buddha and which is worthy to be known as "the perfection of giving."

Bhikshu Vaśitva then concludes his discussion of the perfection of giving with eight stanzas devoted to describing critical distinctions between false and genuine benefactors, noting at the very beginning the prime importance of giving without coveting karmic rewards, with compassion, and without attachment to any of the three factors involved in giving (benefactor, gift, recipient).

False Benefactors

Those benefactors who are attached to the fact that they give or what they have given or who do so with an eye to karmic or social rewards from their giving are described by Bhikshu Vaśitva as not benefactors at all, but "mere businessmen engaged in buying and selling."

Genuine Benefactors

The genuine benefactor is like the great monsoon cloud bringing rain to every place equally. He gives "with heartfelt sympathy," reflecting on recipients "as if they were his own fathers and mothers," while "not retaining in his mind those things which are given, the recipients of the gifts, or the one who does the giving" and while "finding constant happiness in the act of giving." He concludes by stating that the benefactor who gives for the sake of realizing bodhi will succeed in the swift realization of buddhahood.

The Discussion of the Perfection of Moral Virtue

Śīla (moral virtue) has multiple connotations having to do with its functions and effects on the practitioner, these in terms of: habituation, basic nature, coolness, security, quiescence, cessation, stateliness, purity, primacy, and praiseworthiness.

Moral Virtue as Defined by the Ten Good Karmic Deeds

The moral precepts restrain the ten bad karmic actions of body, mouth and mind. (Killing, stealing, sexual misconduct, lying, slanderous speech, harsh speech, frivolous-or-lewd speech, covetousness, hatefulness, wrong views.) Depending on the degree of departure from those standards one becomes vulnerable to descent into the three wretched destinies (hells, animals, *preta* ghosts).

Moral Virtue Generating Enhanced Rebirth Circumstances

Now, so long as coursing in the ten good acts is disconnected from factors generating enlightenment (such as the resolve to follow one of the Buddhist spiritual liberation paths joined to the three trainings: moral virtue, meditation, transcendent wisdom), it generates, depending on degree, various levels of rebirth in human and celestial realms.

Moral Virtue Generating Transcendence of Cyclic Existence

Where linked to enlightenment-generating factors, constant, habitual, and often-repeated coursing in the ten good karmic actions done at the superior level of moral precept practice results in acquisition of stations on the paths of the Śrāvaka-disciples or the Bodhisattvas.

Bodhisattva Precepts

Observance of the bodhisattva moral precept codes has positive effects extending endlessly on in to the future. One should learn more about this matter.

"Continuous" Versus "Discontinuous" Moral Precepts

"Continuous" (lit "same when transplanted") moral precepts are those which carry forward from one life to the next, with consequences of that momentum playing out in terms of one's tendency towards moral virtue, in terms of the quality of rebirth circumstances encountered, in terms of the karmic rewards one spontaneously falls heir to, in terms of the tendency to take up or not take up an individual-liberation path as opposed to a universal-liberation path, in terms of the purelands with which one retains a relationship, and in terms of one's tendency to progress towards right and universal enlightenment.

"Discontinuous" moral virtue is that in which these lifetime-to-lifetime effects do not occur.

"Effortful" Versus "Effortless" Moral Precepts

"Effortful" moral virtue is the circumstance where one must self-monitor intentionality and action to remain in accordance with what is morally correct, whereas "effortless" moral virtue is that wherein one's level of realization has become such that one may act spontaneously without fear of erring.

A Nine-Fold Classification of Moral Precepts

There are yet another nine kinds of moral precepts, as follows:

1) The moral precepts for the common person.
2) The moral precepts of the non-Buddhists who have gained the five spiritual powers.
3) The moral precepts of humans.
4) The moral precepts of the desire-realm gods.
5) The moral precepts of the form-realm gods.
6) The moral precepts of the formless-realm gods.
7) The moral precepts of Śrāvaka-disciples, both those still in training and those beyond training.
8) The moral precepts of the Pratyekabuddhas.
9) The moral precepts of the Bodhisattvas.

(Bhikshu Vaśitva then notes the specific conditions under which the first eight categories of moral precepts terminate, while pointing out that it is only the moral virtue of bodhisattva vows which continue on endlessly from one life to the next.)

It is because the moral-precepts of the Bodhisattvas are dedicated to the realization of the awakening of a buddha that they are said to define "the perfection of moral virtue."

Bhikshu Vaśitva's Verses on the Perfection of Moral Virtue

Bhikshu Vaśitva concludes with a dozen verses in praise of the perfection of moral virtue specifically as they relate to practice in and advancement along the Bodhisattva Path.

The Discussion of the Perfection of Patience

As intended herein, the patience (*kṣānti*) refers to the ability of one's resolve to endure all manner of suffering and bliss, both physical and mental, without feeling either elevated or depressed, and without the mind being clouded by any defilement-induced turbidity. This is a brief description of what is meant by *kṣānti*.

Relying on the interpretation of Bhikshu Vaśitva, one speaks of three types of patience based on the means through which it is sustained: body, mind, or Dharma.

Patience Sustained by the Body

Here, pain is inflicted by either sentient or insentient entities or circumstances, yet one doesn't dwell on it, but rather simply endures the experience peacefully. Examples include:

The pain of hunger from inability to gain sustenance.

Mosquitoes, snakes, tigers, lions, bears, or other two-legged or four-legged beings.

People seeking to cut off hands, feet, ears, nose, head, eyes, or limbs.

Wind, sun, cold, heat, rain, hail, or physical blows.

Any of the various diseases.

Patience Sustained by the Mind

Here, one undergoes challenges mental challenges and yet the mind remains unmoved, neither elevated nor cast down, free of turbid mentation, and free of confusion. Examples include:

Torment, cursing, vilification, denunciation, slander, defamation, deception, and other forms of unenjoyable speech.

The eight worldly dharmas: gain, loss, esteem, disesteem, blame, praise, suffering, and happiness.

One realizes an ability to cease all latent traces of hatefulness, doesn't entertain murderous, injurious, enmity-driven, contentious, or accusatory thoughts, feels protective of both self and others, feels kindness and compassion for others, abides in delight, and courses in equanimity.

Patience Sustained by Dharma

One remains unmoved even in the most challenging cases of physical and mental abuse by resort to a reality-based reflection refuting any reality to the factors involved. One finds no reality in the words and word-borne meanings involved in vilification, finds no reality to a physical body's ability (being mere form) to inflict harm, finds no reality to a mind's ability (being entirely formless) to inflict harm, and finds no reality to a person (being but a mere composite of the five aggregates) supposedly undergoing harm.

Thus one realizes there is no genuine inherent existence to any personal or extrapersonal entity or phenomenon involved in any such circumstances. Thus one abides in the unproduced-dharmas patience which, even in the midst of phenomena, realizes the unreality of all phenomena.

Verses on the Perfection of Patience

Bhikshu Vaśitva then presents ten stanzas on patience, attributed to "an Ārya." The stanzas embody all of the principles set forth in Bhikshu Vaśitva's commentary. (One might be tempted to suppose that "an Ārya" is a reference to Ārya Nāgārjuna but for the fact that Bhikshu Vaśitva's three-part typology of emptiness does not seem to be typical in Nāgārjuna's writings.)

The Discussion of the Perfection of Vigor

Vigor is heroically energetic strength in both the substance and manifest aspects [of one's resolve] and in the performance of karmic works.

The pāramitā of vigor is characterized by the good physical, verbal, and mental karma pursued by bodhisattvas from the time they bring forth their initial resolve on through till that time when they finally reach buddhahood, all of them being carried out in conformance with the factors conducing to enlightenment. It is vigor beyond the sphere of that pursued by common folk, *śrāvakas*, or pratyekabuddhas.

Three Types of Vigor

We refer here to three fundamental categories of vigor: physical, verbal, and mental. Specifically, these actions are:

1) Conducive to the generation of karmic blessings.
2) Beneficial to both self and other.

The Bodhisattvas' Thirty-Two Types of Vigor

1) Vigor in preventing the severance of the lineage of the Three Jewels.
2) Vigor in ripening countless beings.
3) Vigor in drawing in and adopting countless beings entrapped in cyclic existence.
4) Vigor in making countless offerings to support and serve [the Three Jewels].
5) Vigor in accumulating an immeasurable stock of roots of goodness.
6) Vigor in generating an immeasurable reserve of vigor.
7) Vigor in presenting skillful explanations [of Dharma] delightful to beings.
8) Vigor in establishing all beings in secure circumstances.
9) Vigor in adapting to the various endeavors of beings.
10) Vigor in coursing in equanimity in the midst of beings.
11) Vigor in taking on all aspects of the training in moral virtue.
12) Vigor in developing one's power of patience to the point of abiding in mental pliancy.
13) Vigor in acquisition of dhyānas, samādhis, and *samāpattis*.
14) Vigor in perfecting wisdom free of attachment.
15) Vigor in perfecting "the four types of *brahmacarya*" [otherwise known as "the four immeasurable minds"].
16) Vigor in generating the five spiritual powers.
17) Vigor in creating one's own buddhaland based on the qualities present in all other buddhalands.
18) Vigor in subduing all demons.
19) Vigor in subduing in accordance with Dharma all of the non-Buddhist dialecticians.
20) Vigor in perfecting the ten powers, the fearlessnesses, and the other dharmas exclusive to buddhas.
21) Vigor in enhancing the quality of one's physical, verbal, and mental karma.
22) Vigor in completing all endeavors one has begun.

23) Vigor in wreaking destruction on all of one's afflictions.
24) Vigor in escorting beyond [the sea of suffering] all who have not yet gone beyond it.
25) Vigor in causing those not liberated to gain liberation.
26) Vigor in reviving those not yet revived.
27) Vigor in enabling nirvāṇa for those not reaching nirvāṇa.
28) Vigor in accumulating the provisions which generate the [buddha body's] hundred-fold signs of meritorious qualities (*śata-puṇya-lakṣaṇa*).
29) Vigor in gathering in and integrating all buddha dharmas.
30) Vigor in roaming to the boundlessly many buddhalands.
31) Vigor in seeing the immeasurably many buddhas.
32) Vigor in making all such types of vigor issue forth from the great compassion.

The ability to personify such vigor is rooted in transcendent body, mouth, and mind karma, in remaining free of grasping or forsaking, in invulnerability to elation or depression, and in realization that phenomena are not produced at all. Perfection of these dharmas is key to cultivation of the pāramitā of vigor.

Nāgārjuna's Verses on the Perfection of Vigor

Bhikshu Vaśitva presents nine stanzas on vigor, attributed to "the Ārya." Aspects covered include:

1) All other perfections depend on this perfection of vigor.
2) Vigor is the basis for acquisition of a buddha's body.
3) Vigor is supreme among all skillful means.
4) Even skills, wealth, and happiness depend on vigor.
5) Vigor is the essential element in the supremacy of buddhas.

The Discussion of the Perfection of Dhyāna Meditation

The Four Dhyānas

There are four dhyānas, as below:

1) Possessed of primary ideation (*vitarka*), possessed of mental discursion (*vicāra*), and possessed of that joy (*prīti*) and that bliss (*sukha*) that are generated through abandonment, one courses in the first dhyāna.

2) Free of primary ideation, free of mental discursion, and possessed of that joy (*prīti*) and that bliss (*sukha*) that are generated through concentration, one courses in the second dhyāna.

3) Having abandoned joy, possessed of equanimity with respect to karmic formative factors (*saṃskāra-upekṣā*), possessed of mindfulness (*smṛti*), possessed of wise awareness (*saṃprajanya*), and experiencing blissful sensation (*sukha-vedanā*), one courses in the third dhyāna.

4) Having extinguished both suffering and bliss, abiding in equanimity, possessed of purified mindfulness, and experiencing sensations as neither suffering nor blissful, one courses in the fourth dhyāna.

When with respect to these four dhyānas, one has abandoned [the goal of using them as means to gain] realization of the grounds of the Śrāvaka-disciples and the Pratyekabuddhas and has instead dedicated one's efforts in them toward the ground of buddhahood, this qualifies as [practice directed toward] dhyāna pāramitā.

The Sixteen Types of Bodhisattva Dhyāna Pāramitā

There are sixteen types of perfection in dhyāna meditation specific to bodhisattvas and not emphasized in the meditative discipline of the Śrāvakas and the Pratyekabuddhas. Their primary aspects are as follows:

1) Not seizing on anything as real, cultivated to perfect the dhyāna of the Tathāgatas.

2) Refraining from attachment to delectably blissful meditation states, cultivated to avoid attachment to one's own bliss.

3) Implementation of the great compassion to change objective circumstances, cultivated to manifest skillful means capable of halting beings' afflictions.

4) Reversing the direction of samādhi's focus, cultivated to change objective circumstances in the desire realm.

5) Generation of spiritual powers, cultivated to maintain awareness of the mental activity of beings.

6) Development of the mind's capacities, cultivated to perfect the mind's sovereign mastery of wisdom.

7) Development of all *samāpattis*, cultivated to achieve supreme transcendence of the form and formless realms.

8) Abiding in quiescent stillness within quiescent stillness, cultivated to achieve supreme transcendence going beyond the *samāpattis* of *śrāvakas* and pratyekabuddhas.

9) Abiding in immovability, cultivated to reach the most ultimate limit.

10) Employing antidotes to abandon evil, cultivated to destroy the ability of habitual karmic propensities to continue on into the future.

11) Entering wisdom, cultivated to transcend all mundane realms.

12) Adaptation to beings' mental actions, cultivated to facilitate the liberation of beings.

13) Preventing interruption of the Three Jewels lineage, cultivated to ensure the never-ending continuance of the dhyānas originating with the Tathāgatas.

14) Invulnerability to retreating or falling, cultivated through constant immersion in samādhi.

15) Sovereign mastery in all dharmas, cultivated to achieve perfect consummation of all of one's karmic works.

16) Analytic deconstruction of entities, [cultivated to counter baseless imputations of intrinsic existence].

The Thirty-Two Types of Purity Forming the Bases of Dhyāna

In addition, there are the thirty-two types of purity serving as the bases for development of the sixteen kinds of dhyāna and hence for progress on the path to buddhahood:

1) Purity in thought.
2) Purity in wisdom.
3) Purity in [the nature of] one's inclinations.
4) Purity inhering in possessing a sense of shame.
5) Purity in the aspirations sustaining the mind.
6) Purity associated with dedication [of merit] to bodhi.
7) Purity in one's faculties.
8) Purity associated with freedom from dependencies.
9) Purity associated with not seizing upon anything as real.
10) Purity associated with the generation and implementation of spiritual powers.
11) Purity in exercising the capacities of the mind.
12) Purity associated with physical renunciation.
13) Purity associated with inward stillness.
14) Purity associated with refraining from external activity.
15) Purity in one's views regarding perceptual apprehensibility.
16) Purity through realization of the nonexistence of any being.
17) Purity through realization of the nonexistence of any life.
18) Purity through realization of the nonexistence of persons.

19) Purity associated with having nowhere in the three realms in which one abides.

20) Purity associated with the methods comprised by the factors conducive to enlightenment.

21) Purity associated with the illumination through which one abandons the obscurations.

22) Purity associated with entry into wisdom.

23) Purity associated with having no inconsistencies regarding karmic cause-and-effect.

24) Purity associated with bringing patience to one's contemplations on karma.

25) Purity inherent in realizing the wisdom fathoming all aspects of the womb [from which buddhahood is born].

26) Purity associated with the preliminary expedient means used to attract [beings onto the Path].

27) Purity associated with avoiding obstructiveness within any site dedicated to the realization of bodhi.

28) Purity associated with refraining from attachment to [dharmas of] the Śrāvaka-disciples and the Pratyekabuddhas.

29) Purity associated with the radiance generated when peacefully abiding in dhyāna.

30) Purity inhering in the freedom from mental scatteredness associated with the samādhis of the Buddha.

31) Purity associated with contemplating the behavior of one's own mind.

32) Purity associated with speaking Dharma well-suited to beings based on awareness of the karmic origins of each and every one of them.

Bhikshu Vaśitva's Concluding Verse on Dhyāna Pāramitā and the Powers

Bhikshu Vaśitva concludes this discussion with eight stanzas in which he:

1)   Notes that the sixteen types of dhyāna pāramitā correspond to the perfection of dhyāna meditation when they are cultivated for the sake of realizing bodhi.

2)   Notes that the wise use the powers in service of ensuring invulnerability to retreating from or falling away from the Path.

3)   Describes the bodhisattva's use of heavenly eye, heavenly ear, knowledge of others' thoughts, knowledge of past lives and abodes, and mastery of spiritual power to travel to countless buddhalands.

4)   Notes that the wise, realizing that the scattered mind is the root of all afflictions, extensively cultivate the dhyāna absorptions.

—————

The Discussion of the Perfection of Wisdom

Having already extensively discussed the perfection of wisdom earlier in the commentary, Bhikshu Vaśitva simply reiterates here that it is foremost among all provisions essential to bodhi and that it subsumes all of the other perfections. He then defines the perfection of wisdom as "that single thought-moment of comprehensive wisdom through which the Buddha, the Bhagavān, awakened to the nature of all dharmas as he sat beneath the Bodhi Tree."

Bhikshu Vaśitva then provides a list of twenty aspects associated with the perfection of wisdom:

It is unimpeded because it is independent of the body.

It is boundless because it is as vast as empty space.

It is equal to the unequaled because, in it, no dharma is perceptually apprehensible.

It is characterized by renunciation because of the ultimate emptiness [of all phenomena].

It is unconquerable because nothing whatsoever can be gotten at in it.

It is completely devoid of any sentence-based propositions because designations themselves are nonexistent entities.

It is devoid of any aggregation [of subsidiary components] because it transcends all coming hither and going thither.

It is free of any cause because it abandons [the concept of] any creative agent.

It is unproduced because production itself cannot be established as existing.

It involves no going anywhere because it has abandoned coursing in cyclic existence.

It is free of any disintegration because it transcends beginnings and endings.

It is stainless because it cannot even be grasped.

It is free of any frivolous discoursing because it has abandoned all frivolous discoursing.

It is unshakable because it is identical with the very substance of the entire Dharma realm.

It involves no arising because it does not engage in any discriminations.

It is immeasurable because it has transcended all modes of measurement.

It is free of any points of dependence because dependency itself does not exist.

It is free of defilement because it does not even come forth into existence.

It is unfathomable because it has no confining boundaries.

It is spontaneous through knowing the nature of all dharmas.

Additionally, it is marked by eighty kinds of wisdom derived from learning, thirty-two kinds of accessibility through right meditation, and freedom from sixteen kinds of delusion.

This treatment of the aspects of prajñāpāramitā is limited in its extent. Were one were to attempt to explain them completely, one would find they are limitless.

––––––––

The Discussion of the Perfection of Skillful Means

The Eight Varieties of Skillful Means

The pāramitā of skillful means is comprised of eight categories:

1) Skillful means related to the [five] aggregates.
2) Skillful means related to the [eighteen] sense realms.
3) Skillful means related to the [six] sense bases.
4) Skillful means related to the [four] truths.
5) Skillful means related to conditioned arising.
6) Skillful means related to the three periods of time.
7) Skillful means related to the vehicles [for liberation].
8) Skillful means related to dharmas.

The Scope of What Should Be Explained Herein

The applications of skillful means in these spheres are boundlessly many. The great eminences have explained in detail what is appropriate according to rebirth destiny and applicable cultivation modes as one simultaneously augments one's own goodness and works to train beings. We describe below but a tiny drop of what is mentioned in the Sutras on this topic.

Skillful Means as Whatever Increases Goodness and Stems from Altruism

If a person's karma involves past or present goodness and one is able to cause its increase, doing so not for self-serving purposes, but rather to benefit of others, this qualifies as skillful means.

The Six Perfections as Skillful Means

One may use giving to facilitate fulfillment of the perfections, may use moral virtue to draw in beings, may use patience to enhance one's karma and assist acquisition of bodhi, may resort to vigor to generate energetic progress, may cultivate meditation to prevent loss of the dhyāna absorptions, or may cultivate wisdom to relinquish attachment to the unconditioned. In such cases, each of the perfections qualifies as a valid skillful means.

The Four Immeasurable Minds as Skillful Means

One may cultivate kindness to become a refuge and protector for beings, may devote oneself to compassion so as to avoid forsaking those trapped in cyclic existence, may cultivate sympathetic joy to endure unenjoyable circumstances, or may train in equanimity as the means to develop every manner of goodness.

The Spiritual Powers as Skillful Means

One uses the heavenly eye to facilitate acquisition of the buddha eye, uses the heavenly ear to perfect the hearing capacities of a buddha, uses knowledge of others' thoughts to know the faculties of beings, uses past-life recall to gain unimpeded knowledge of the three periods of time, uses sovereign mastery of spiritual powers to gain the Tathāgatas' sovereign mastery of spiritual powers, and uses access to beings' thoughts to understand their actions.

Seemingly Paradoxical Skillful Means of Bodhisattvas in Cyclic Existence

Having already achieved liberation, one may turn and enter cyclic existence yet again, having become free of defilement, may become exposed to defilement, having thrown down all burdens, may voluntarily take up burdens, having reached the limitless, may manifest as limited, and, having reached supremacy, may nonetheless manifest as possessing merely inferior capacities.

Having gained realizations equivalent to nirvāṇa, one may drop back into cyclic existence and, though coursing in this realization of nirvāṇa, one abstains from entering final cessation.

Though one may find it necessary to manifest practice associated with the four types of demon-related influences [involving afflictions, the aggregates, death, and sixth desire heaven deities], one continues to entirely transcend every form of demonic influence. Though realizing wisdom utterly fathoming the four truths, and though coursing in contemplation of the unproduced, one abstains from entering the point of no return leading to *śrāvaka*-vehicle nirvāṇa.

Though cultivating the Path in the very midst of cyclic existence's vexing boisterousness, one refrains from actions rooted in latent afflictions. Though coursing in renunciation, one refrains from practice precipitating complete cessation of body and mind. Though one abides in the midst of the three realms, one nonetheless refrains from practice dominated by worldly truth.

Though one's practice is rooted in emptiness, one focuses on the quest for buddhahood. Though one courses in the unconditioned, one avoids opting for realization of the unconditioned. Though one develops the six spiritual powers, one refrains from ending all outflow impurities. Though one manifests the refined comportment of *śrāvaka* disciples and pratyekabuddhas, one does not relinquish delight and zeal for the dharmas of a buddha.

Such are the practices involved in the perfection of skillful means utilized by bodhisattvas in their teaching of beings.

(Bhikshu Vaśitva's full-length commentary concludes with thirteen stanzas describing in rich detail the skillful-means practices of the great bodhisattvas. They are omitted here due to space considerations.)

The Discussion of the Perfection of Vows

All bodhisattvas establish themselves from the very outset in the ten great vows, namely:

(Bhikshu Vaśitva does not make even one original statement in this section, preferring instead to simply quote the *Avataṃsaka Sutra* on the ten bodhisattva vows. That being the case, I've set that aside in favor of simply translating and inserting below Nāgārjuna's much clearer and much more concise distillation of these vows in stanzas from his *Ten Grounds Vibhāṣā*.)

[1] One vows to make offerings to, supply the needs of,
And extend reverence to all buddhas.
[2] One vows that in all cases one will protect and uphold
The Dharma of all buddhas.

[3] From that time when all Buddhas depart the Tuṣita Heaven
And come back to abide in the world,
On forward to the end of their teaching and transforming
And eternal entry into the realm of [the nirvāṇa] without residue,

Including when they abide in the womb, on up to their birth,
On to their leaving lay life, proceeding to the site of enlightenment,
Their conquering the demons, realizing the path to buddhahood,
And their first turning of the wheel of the sublime Dharma—

I will respectfully welcome all of the Tathāgatas,
And throughout that entire time—
I vow that in all cases I shall
Be entirely devoted to making offerings to them.

[4] I vow to teach and transform beings,
Causing them all to enter the paths.
[5] I vow to influence all beings
To perfect the bodhi of the Buddhas,

[Including] where they incline toward the Śrāvaka-disciple
Or Pratyekabuddha paths.
[6] I vow that, through faith and understanding,
I shall realize the uniform equality of all dharmas.

[7] I vow that, in order to purify the buddhalands,
I shall extinguish all of the various forms of evil.
[8] Where all are engaged in the practice of a single endeavor,
One vows that there will be no enmity or struggling.

[9] One vows to practice the Bodhisattva Path
And to set to turning that irreversible wheel,
Thus causing the removal of all afflictions
And fulfilling success in entering the state of purified faith.

[10] One vows that, in all worlds,
One shall manifest the realization of bodhi.
All such bodhisattvas as these
Take the ten great vows as foremost.

In their immense vastness, they are comparable to empty space
And exhaust even the bounds of the future.
They entirely include all of the other incalculably many vows
And exhaust as well one's ability to describe them all in detail.

Great vows such as these ten characterized by great zeal and
great manifestations in the world comprise the foremost class of
vows. After one has fulfilled these ten great vows, one establishes
asaṃkhyeyas of hundreds of thousands of other bodhisattva vows.
Thus one comes to abide on the bodhisattva's "ground of joyfulness" (*pramudita-bhūmi*). This exemplifies what is meant by the perfection of vows.

The Discussion of the Perfection of Powers

Generally speaking, the Bodhisattvas possess seven kinds of powers, as follows:

1) The power produced through karmic reward.
2) The power of the supernatural powers.
3) The power of faith.
4) The power of vigor.
5) The power of mindfulness.
6) The power of the samādhis.
7) The power of prajñā.

The Power Produced Through Karmic Reward

This refers to the inconceivable and ineffable power deriving from the altruistic deeds done across the course of countless eons of coursing in the bodhisattva path.

The Power of the Supernatural Powers

This refers to a broad range of spiritual powers employed by bodhisattvas once they have successfully cultivated to refinement the four bases of spiritual power (zeal, vigor, single-mindedness, imaginative reflective thought).

Once developed, the bodhisattva is able to manifest among other beings in whatever form might most readily advance those beings along the path to liberation from karma-bound suffering in cyclic existence. Thus, they may manifest in the form of Śakra, Brahmā, a world-protector, a universal monarch, or in some other such physical form. If it be appropriate that they appear in yet another type of physical form, even to the point of manifesting in the physical form of an animal, this for the sake of training beings, then they manifest in just such a physical form.

The spiritual powers of the bodhisattvas include the ability to perform whatever miraculous feats might suit their altruistic purposes. Thus, if there be an arrogant being of overweening pride, one who is prone to hateful rages and who is cruel, evil, and self-important, then the bodhisattvas are able to employ their spiritual powers as the circumstance requires, thus being able to successfully speak Dharma for them, thus training and subduing them, causing them thereby to abandon their arrogance, overweening pride, hateful rages, cruelty, evil, and such.

In this manner, if they have some manifestation of spiritual power which they have invoked, then no matter what they have invoked, whether it be a lesser, middling, or superior sort of dharma, having already succeeded in invoking it, it becomes such as no person is able to disturb or cause to disappear. This is to say then that even if it were Śakra, Brahmā, a demon, or someone from another world system possessed of identical dharmas, aside from a buddha, one of the Bhagavāns, there is no being whatsoever anywhere among all of the classes of beings that would be able to disturb that manifestation of spiritual powers or cause it to disappear.

In their exercise of the power of spiritual powers, they invoke them with sovereign mastery at the highest level. They go beyond the afflictions produced through the influence of demons and enter into that very state of mind possessed by the Buddhas themselves. They employ such powers in the awakening of beings and in the accumulation of the provisions for the acquisition of bodhi, bringing to bear the roots of goodness accumulated across the course of previous lives. These powers are such as the demons and the demonically-influenced celestial beings are unable to impede. This is what constitutes "the power of the supernatural powers" possessed by the Bodhisattvas.

The Power of Faith

As for "the power of faith," they possess such faith and understanding in the Buddha, the Dharma, the Sangha, and the Bodhisattva Conduct as can never be obstructed or damaged.

The Power of Vigor

As for "the power of vigor," in an instance where the bodhisattva invokes his practice of vigor, in whichever of those good dharmas to which it is applied, he succeeds in gaining in just such circumstances the power of enduring solidity of practice. No matter which practice he has undertaken, no god or person is able to shake him in that practice, damage that practice, or cause him to cease that practice.

The Power of Mindfulness

As for "the power of mindfulness," in whichever of those various dharmas his mind has become established, no extraneous afflictive circumstance is able to cause him to become scattered. Through the sustaining power of mindfulness, he is able to break all afflictions. Thus none of those afflictions are able to break or cause the deterioration of the bodhisattva's mindfulness.

The Power of the Samādhis

As for "the power of samādhi," even in the midst of vexing boisterousness, he continues to course in renunciation of worldly matters. Thus extraneous noise or conversations do not impede his coursing in the first dhyāna, ideation and discursion do not impede his coursing in the second dhyāna, blissful states do not impede his coursing in the third dhyāna, and his ripening of beings and acquisition of Path-related dharmas do not impede his coursing in the fourth dhyāna. Evil opposing states encountered in the practice of the dhyānas remain unable to damage or undermine his practice and, though he courses in the dhyānas, he nonetheless refrains from taking rebirth in those celestial realms corresponding to the dhyānas.

The Power of Prajñā

As for "the power of prajñā," this refers to wisdom which remains undamaged even in the midst of all manner of worldly and world-transcending dharmas. In life after life, he is so able to remain wisely guided by prajñā that he need not resort to the teachings of a guru.

All sorts of livelihoods, all of the arts and skills, all of the abilities in the higher clarities, and even the world's most supreme, most difficult, and most difficult to endure abilities—the bodhisattva has them all manifest for him as abilities he is free to exercise. In the case of those world-transcending dharmas with which one rescues and liberates beings in the world, once the bodhisattva's wisdom has entered into them, they become such as no group of gods, men, or *asuras* can overturn or interfere with.

This has been only a summary treatment of the powers in which the bodhisattva develops sovereign mastery. A complete discussion would be endless.

The Discussion of the Perfection of Knowledges

The bodhisattva develops a deep understanding not just of the world-transcending skills, but also of the skills useful in the world. Thus he understands classics, philosophical treatises, printing, mathematics, medicine, exorcism, the means to counter poisonings inflicted through black magic, and so forth.

He has a skillful command of humor and satire as means to delight beings, making them more amenable to Dharma teaching.

He knows how to establish public works, including correct city planning, water projects, parks, gardens, orchards, and forestry.

He is familiar with metallurgy, precious gems, and so forth.

He understands astronomy, constellations, eclipses, seismology, augury through dreams, and physiognomy.

He understands the points of practice associated with the moral precepts, the meditative absorptions, the spiritual powers, the four immeasurables, and the formless realm stations.

He understands the arising and destruction of worlds and the role that individual and group karma play therein.

He also understands the most minute particles, how they join in compounds, how they disperse, and even how many of them there are in any particular sphere.

He understands the arising and destruction of the desire realm, form realm, and formless realm.

He knows in great detail the distinctions in the form and formless bodies of the various classes of beings on each of the paths.

He knows the matters associated with the establishment of the Buddhas, the Dharma, and the Ārya Sangha

Additionally, he has succeeded in gaining sovereign mastery of the lifespan, mind, equipage, karmic actions, vows, faith and understanding, spiritual powers, knowledges, rebirths, and Dharma.

Having gained ten such types of sovereign mastery, he then becomes one possessed of inconceivable and ineffable knowledges, becomes one possessed of immeasurably many knowledges, and becomes one possessed of the knowledges whereby he remains invulnerable to retreating from the path to buddhahood. Knowledges of these sorts involve eighty-four thousand practice-related aspects. It is this which constitutes the pāramitā of the knowledges known by the bodhisattva.

We have presented in this fashion a categorized explanation of the pāramitā of the knowledges. If one wished to expound on the matter completely, it would be only the Buddha, the Bhagavān, who would be qualified to present that explanation.

007 – The Six Perfections, Like Space, Comprehensively Subsume Bodhi's Provisions

These six pāramitās
Encompass the provisions essential for bodhi,
They are comparable in this to empty space
Which entirely envelopes all things.

AV These six perfections completely contain all of the various sorts of requisites for realization of bodhi in just the same way that empty space contains all conscious and unconscious phenomena abiding within it.

008 – Another Exegete's Opinion: The Four Merit Bases Subsume All Provisions

There is also the idea proposed by another master
That, as for the provisions for enlightenment,
Truth, relinquishment, cessation, and wisdom—
These four bases subsume them all.

AV "Truth" here is identifiable with the perfection of moral virtue, "relinquishment" with the perfection of giving, "cessation" with the perfections of patience and meditation, and "wisdom" with the perfection of prajñā. The perfection of vigor is present in all of these bases, for without it, nothing at all would be accomplished.

TN The four "bases" (*adhiṣṭhāna*) consist of "truth" (*satya*), "relinquishment" (*tyāga*), "cessation" (*upaśama*), and "wisdom" (*prajñā*).

Nāgārjuna speaks highly of these four bases in a number of his works, most notably in the *Ratnāvalī*, in his treatise on the ten bodhisattva grounds, and in his *Exegesis on the Great Perfection of Wisdom Sutra*. The four bases are also found in the Pali Canon, for example in the *Dhātuvibhanga Sutta* within the *Majjhima Nikāya*.

009 – The Great Compassion and the Great Kindness

The great compassion penetrates to the marrow of one's bones.
Thus one serves as a refuge for every being.
With a feeling as strong as a father's regard for his only son,
One's kindness extends universally to all beings.

TN This *śloka* and the two which follow are devoted primarily to the four immeasurable minds consisting of kindness, compassion, sympathetic joy, and equanimity.

AV The bodhisattva observes the pathetic plight of beings trapped in the forest of delusions and bound to undergo endless suffering. Observing this, the bodhisattva is so pierced by the pangs of the great compassion that those feelings penetrate even to his very bones. He is motivated thereby to serve as a refuge for beings, striving to lead them out of the wilderness of cyclic existence into the city of enlightenment.

The feelings of the bodhisattva for beings are like that of a father whose only son has fallen seriously ill. It is through kindness that one frees oneself from any inclination to be obstructive of other beings' aspirations and it is through compassion that one remains free of weariness or disgust while working in the sphere of cyclic existence for the weal of beings.

Kindness is generated toward the good whereas compassion is felt even for those who show no goodness. As the bodhisattva's kindness grows ever greater, he becomes detached from any concerns over his own happiness, hence "the great kindness." As his compassion grows ever greater, he becomes willing to sacrifice everything for others, hence "the great compassion."

---

010 – The Great Sympathetic Joy

If one brings to mind the qualities of a buddha
Or hears of a buddha's spiritual transformations,
One becomes purified through one's admiration and joyfulness.
This is what is meant by the great sympathetic joy.

AV As for "qualities of a buddha," Bhikshu Vaśitva lists thirty-three which should inspire admiration and joy in those who contemplate them. He then follows by explaining the Buddhas' use of "spiritual transformations" in adapting to the different sorts of beings and in formulating skillful means to teach them. Bhikshu Vaśitva then describes how admiration generates sympathetic joy and how sympathetic joy brings about an absence of turbidity in the mind corresponding to karmic purification while then noting in conclusion that, although lesser-scope vehicles include the concept of "sympathetic joy," they do not share the level of development spoken of here which, being in a class by itself, is alone in qualifying as "the great sympathetic joy."

011 – The Great Equanimity

In his relations with beings, the bodhisattva
Should not allow himself to forsake them.
As befits the abilities determined by his powers,
He should always strive to draw them in.

AV The bodhisattva, *mahāsattva*, remains motivated to benefit beings and make them happy. Thus, even where they behave abysmally, one should refrain from forsaking them. Rather, one should persist in encouraging them to cultivate giving and moral virtue. In accordance with one's abilities, one should strive to draw them in [to the Path].

012 – The Role of Skillful Means

From the very beginning, the bodhisattva
Should accord with the power of his abilities
And use skillful means to instruct beings,
Causing them to enter the Great Vehicle.

AV As he interacts with beings, consistent with the earlier explanation of the perfection of skillful means, the bodhisattva should energetically employ expedients causing beings to enter the Great Vehicle. Bhikshu Vaśitva then introduces the next *śloka* with a hypothetical challenging question: Why does the bodhisattva initially use only Great Vehicle teachings in this endeavor?

013 – The Superior Merit Arising from Teaching the Great Vehicle

Even if one taught beings as numerous as the Ganges' sands
So that they were caused to gain the fruit of arhatship,
Still, by instructing but a single person to enter the Great Vehicle,
One would generate merit superior to that.

AV The merit arising from teaching the Great Vehicle is supreme because the karmic seeds planted thereby are inexhaustible in their secondary effects, this because they redound to the benefit of yet other beings, thus constituting expedients inspiring their resolve to gain the highest enlightenment. Additionally, the mind resolved on bodhi possesses innumerable fine qualities. Moreover, it is solely via the Great Vehicle that the lineage of the Three Jewels is not severed completely [during the Dharma-ending age].

Bhikshu Vaśitva introduces the next *śloka* with a theoretical challenging question: "How could it be that *mahāsattvas* would teach only the Great Vehicle, never using Two-Vehicles teachings?"

---

014 – The Two Vehicles Are Taught Only to Those of Lesser Abilities

Instructing through resort to the Śrāvaka Vehicle
Or through resort to the Pratyekabuddha Vehicle
Is undertaken where, on account of lesser abilities,
Beings are unable to accept instruction in the Great Vehicle.

AV Beings of lesser resolve have forsaken the benefit of others and hence are deficient in the great compassion. Consequently one can't use the Great Vehicle to teach them. Only then does one resort to Two-Vehicles teachings to teach liberation.

Bhikshu Vaśitva introduces the next *śloka* with a question: Does one just abandon those not amenable to any of the Three-Vehicles teachings?

---

015 – Teach Meritorious Deeds to Those Incapable of the Three Vehicles

Where even when relying on Śrāvaka or Pratyekabuddha Vehicles
In addition to the Great Vehicle teachings,
There are those who still cannot accept any such instruction,
One should strive to establish them in merit-creating situations.

AV For those delighting in cyclic existence and abhorring a life devoted to achieving spiritual liberation, one should establish them in practices associated with "the four abodes of Brahmā" (*brahma-vihāra*).

Where not even this is possible, one establishes them in the path of the ten types of good karma, or if that is not tenable, in merit-generating endeavors such as giving.

Bhikshu Vaśitva introduces the next *śloka* with a question: What should one do for beings delighting in worldly pleasures devoid of any strength to adopt merit-generating practices?

TN When Bhikshu Vaśitva speaks of "the four abodes of Brahmā," consisting of kindness, compassion, sympathetic joy, and equanimity, one should note per Nāgārjuna's explanation in his *Exegesis on the Great Perfection of Wisdom Sutra*, that lesser-level practice of these contemplations is as contemplations pure and simple, for they do not genuinely involve or even aspire to involve practices devoted to liberating other beings. This is equally true of śrāvaka-vehicle practice and the practice of worldlings aspiring to achieve rebirth in celestial realms. In śrāvaka-vehicle practice, these contemplations are undertaken solely to condition the mind in a way whereby it is not prone to generate the bad karma arising from afflictions felt for other beings.

The Mahāyāna approach to these four practices differs completely. They are known in the Mahāyāna context as "the four immeasurable minds" (*apramāṇa-citta*). Therein, the bodhisattva practitioner definitely *does* aspire to liberate beings through cultivation of these four immeasurables and in fact relies upon them as foundational contemplations enabling his endless efforts on behalf of other beings.

Bhikshu Vaśitva's recommendation of these practices here arises from the knowledge that beings who take them on will generate less bad karma and will therefore be less likely to plunge so efficiently into the lower realms as those beings who do not adopt such salutary states of mind. Hence we see in that a certain kinship with the śrāvaka-vehicle cultivation rationale. Additionally, since many worldlings do in fact aspire to the bliss of the heavens, this stratagem may be more readily adopted by those viewing practices directed at liberation as too difficult or beyond their powers of faith.

---

016 – Benefit and Slowly Draw in Those Unfit for Liberation or Celestial Rebirth

If there be persons unable to accept
Instruction conducing either to the heavens or to liberation,
Favor them through bestowing present-life benefits.
Then, as befits one's powers, one should draw them in.

AV For beings who are exclusively dedicated to desire-based pleasures, who are ignorant of retribution in future lifetimes, who are bound for the three wretched rebirth destinies, and who are unable to take on teachings conducing to either liberation or the heavens, one should still feel pity for them, instead using giving and other skillful means appealing to their present-life priorities, this so they might slowly be attracted to the Path.

017 – One Generates Kindness and Compassion for Those One Cannot Assist

Where, with regard to particular beings, a bodhisattva
Has no conditions through which to instruct them,
He should draw forth the great kindness and compassion
And should refrain from abandoning them.

AV When encountering beings delighting in karmic transgressions, the bodhisattva should look upon them as he would his own sons and still draw on the great kindness and compassion, realizing there is no rationale condoned by the Path justifying their abandonment.

018 – The Means of Attraction

Drawing them in through giving, through explaining Dharma,
Through listening to them discuss the Dharma,
Or through endeavors beneficial to them—
These are skillful means through which to attract them.

AV As means to attract beings to the Path, the bodhisattva may give gifts, accept gifts, explain Dharma, listen to Dharma, engage in beneficial actions, speak in a pleasing manner, take up joint endeavors, explain specialized fields of learning, teach special skills, manifest as engaged in the same livelihood, cure the sick, or rescue those in perilous straits.

TN One might wonder how "listening to them discuss the Dharma" makes sense where the individuals involved clearly don't well understand the Dharma. This allows the bodhisattva: a) to precisely evaluate the conceptual errors the speaker has developed regarding the Dharma; b) to engage amicably with the speaker on the main topic of concern; and c) to indicate personal respect and concern for the speaker, no matter how skewed their views might be. This helps provide a foundation for friendship based on Dharma.

019 – The Need for Tirelessness, Vows, Realization that Other-Benefit is Self-Benefit

In that which is done for the benefit of beings,
Do not succumb to either weariness or negligence.
Bring forth vows for the sake of realizing bodhi.
Benefiting the world is just benefiting self.

AV The bodhisattva vows: "Whatever endeavors might benefit the world—that is precisely what I should do," and, having made this vow, he must not fall into weariness or negligence. Rather, he should reflect: "When one benefits the world, one is thereby just benefiting oneself as well." Thus the bodhisattva should avoid abandoning beings.

---

020 – Entering the Dharma Realm, Discriminations Cease, Equanimity Ensues

Entering the extremely profound Dharma-realm,
One extinguishes mental discriminations.
As they are devoid of any useful function,
In all contexts, one naturally abides in equanimity.

AV The "Dharma realm" is synonymous with the very nature of the entire sphere of conditioned arising which is itself extremely profound and accurately apprehensible only through extremely profound levels of awareness.

The bodhisattva entering the mind-state cognizing this extremely profound Dharma realm thereby extinguishes all such duality-based extremes as "existence," "non-existence," and so forth. One severs all mind-moving frivolous discourse and mental discriminations, thus one abandons all seizing on any aspects of objective phenomena.

Where the intellectual mind consciousness would ordinarily be active, it ceases to be active. When this occurs, [mental discriminations] no longer serve any function. In the midst of dharmas, one realizes a mind state marked by stillness within stillness, a mind state devoid of mental discriminations. This is the "equanimity conforming to ultimate truth (*paramārtha*)."

---

021 – Equanimity as Remaining Unimpeded by the Eight Worldly Dharmas

Personal gain, reputation, praise, and happiness—
One refrains from attachment to any of these four points.
Nor do their opposites present any sort of obstacle.
This is the sort of conduct comprising equanimity.

AV One retains no attachment to concerns over the receipt of beneficial gains, fame, praise, or happiness. Nor is one inclined to retreat or find any obstacle in the opposite conditions involving loss, ill repute, disparagement, or suffering. One relinquishes both fondness and loathing. One abides in the midst of such conditions and yet remains free of any mental discriminations. This is what is meant by the second type: "equanimity amidst of the mundane."

TN Nāgārjuna references "the eight worldly dharmas," also known as "the eight winds." These eight dharmas are: gain and loss; disgrace and esteem; praise and blame; suffering and happiness.

---

022 – The Need for Diligence So Long as Irreversibility Hasn't Been Gained

So long as he has not yet gained irreversibility,
In the bodhisattva's striving for bodhi,
He should be as intensely diligent in practice
As someone whose turban has caught on fire.

AV Although the bodhisattva abides in transcendent equanimity eschewing mental discriminations, he is nonetheless intensely vigorous in his practice aimed at achieving "irreversibility" in the quest for the enlightenment of a buddha.

As noted in sutras such as the *Accumulation of Blossoms Sutra*, there are basically five circumstances conferring either a relative or ultimate "irreversibility" preventing one from falling away from the path to buddhahood:

1) Hearing the names of buddhas or bodhisattvas equipped with great vows;

2) Making the vow to take rebirth in a buddha's pureland;

3) Accepting, bearing in mind, or discoursing on profound sutras such as those dedicated to the perfection of wisdom;

4) Cultivating samādhis associated with the "direct presence" bodhisattva ground (*abhimukha-bhūmi*) or cultivating sympathetic joy in someone else's realization of such samādhis; and

5) Realization of the "unproduced-dharmas patience" (*anutpattika-dharma-kṣānti*) bringing residence on the "unmoving" bodhisattva ground (*acala-bhūmi*), the eighth bodhisattva ground. Only this fifth type constitutes the "ultimate and definite irreversibility" ensuring future buddhahood.

Bhikshu Vaśitva's discussion of this *śloka* concludes with a question as to how the practitioner could feel compelled to intensely vigorous practice, given the relative ease with which one would have already set up one or more of the first four circumstances producing relative irreversibility.

---

023 – Bodhisattvas' Ceaseless Vigor in Seeking Bodhi Is Due to Heavy Responsibility

Thus it is that those bodhisattvas,
When striving for the realization of bodhi,
Should not rest in their practice of vigor,
For they have shouldered such a heavy burden.

AV The bodhisattva continues on with vigor primarily because of the heavy burden implicit in his bodhisattva vow to deliver all beings to spiritual liberation. The next *śloka* is introduced with a question as to why a bodhisattva can't allow himself to rest during the interim.

---

024 – Prior to Compassion and Patience, the Bodhisattva Life Remains Imperiled

Until one develops the great compassion and the patiences,
Even though he may have gained irreversibility,
The bodhisattva is still subject to a form of "dying"
Occurring through the arising of negligence.

AV So long as the bodhisattva hasn't yet developed the great compassion or realized the unproduced-dharmas patience, even when having already gained the relative irreversibility conferred by any of the first four circumstances mentioned above, he is still vulnerable to the power of his karma and to the destructive power of negligence. Were negligence allowed to arise, it could precipitate the "death" of the bodhisattva life. Hence the need for unremitting and intense vigor.

The next *śloka* is introduced with a question as to what precisely is meant by this "death" to which a bodhisattva is vulnerable.

TN There are two issues deserving amplification here: 1) "patiences"; 2) "irreversibility."

1) On "patiences": The whole topic of the various types of "patiences" realized in Buddhist cultivation is not nearly so simple as one might suspect, this because there are multiple types of patience associated with the sixteen mental states of comprehension involved in developing the Path of Seeing. (See Chapter Six of Vasubandhu's *Abhidharmakośa-bhāṣyam* for a tour of the topic.)

Additionally, in explaining the bodhisattva practices, Nāgārjuna speaks in place after place and at great length on two types of patience: 1) patience with respect to beings; and 2) patience with respect to dharmas. (See Chapter Three of my translation titled *Nāgārjuna on the Six Perfections*.)

Moreover, Bhikshu Vaśitva himself speaks of three basic kinds of patience, this based on three bases of patience found in the body, in the mind, and in the Dharma.

That said, Bhikshu Vaśitva indicates that, in this context, "patiences" refers specifically to the "unproduced dharmas patience" (*anutpattika-dharma-kṣānti*). As an aid to making sense of the topic, "patience" of this sort may be provisionally understood as that type of deeply patient "acquiescence" which one may develop toward coursing in cyclic existence. This can only really come about once one has gained the direct perception of the emptiness of all dharmas. This cognition of emptiness has the ability to engender a continuous perception that, surface appearances aside, all dharmas are, in their most essential nirvāṇa-like nature, neither produced nor destroyed. It is this level of cognition and acquiescence which, when linked to the great compassion, figures most strongly in the bodhisattva's ability to continue on endlessly and selflessly, working for the liberation of other beings.

2) On "irreversibility": It has so far remained unclear in the Bhikshu Vaśitva commentary that, although this "irreversibility" associated with the first four causal circumstances does constitute a virtual guarantee that enlightenment will be gained sooner or later, still, that particular "enlightenment" which awaits the practitioner might not in fact be the enlightenment of a buddha. It could end up being the individual-liberation result gained by those who do not cultivate the altruistic path of the bodhisattva.

How could this occur? If the bodhisattva falls into negligence, he risks a precipitous plunge back down into the śrāvaka or pratyeka-buddha practice modes where the population of beings liberated may be but very few. Hence the reference to the terminal nature of such a downfall, one by which it is metaphorically compared to a tragic death. Certainly not all deaths are "tragic," but those involving being cut off in the flower of a promising youth may justifiably be seen as such. Here we have the prospect of a beginning bodhisattva full of promise and great aspirations losing his grip and plummeting to his death while still only "young" in the practices, thus leaving countless beings bereft of the benefits of his unrealized buddhahood. Hence the appropriateness of the metaphor.

---

025 – Falling onto the Śrāvaka or Pratyekabuddha Grounds is Fatal for a Bodhisattva

The grounds of the Śrāvakas or the Pratyekabuddhas,
If entered, constitute "death" for him
Because he would thereby sever the roots
Of the bodhisattva's understanding and awareness.

AV Even if possessed of "relative" irreversibility, the bodhisattva resolve of one who has not yet gained unproduced-dharmas patience could still succumb to bad friends, to terror over the sufferings involved in cyclic births and deaths, to rebirth in unfortunate circumstances between buddhas, or to hatred of bodhisattvas or slander of right Dharma during the deterioration of the kalpa. The consequence of this might well be diversion onto the paths of the Śrāvaka disciples or the Pratyekabuddhas. This would involve severance of the roots of bodhisattvahood through the ending pursuit of the great compassion. Hence the identification of such a circumstance with the "death" of an individual practitioner's coursing in the Bodhisattva Path.

The next *śloka* is introduced with a question as to whether a bodhisattva would be more struck with fear by the prospect of falling into the hells or instead by the prospect of falling down onto the grounds occupied by the Śrāvaka disciples and the Pratyekabuddhas.

---

026 – The Bodhisattva Fears the Two-Vehicles' Grounds More Than the Hells

At the prospect of falling into the hell-realms,
The bodhisattva would not be struck with fright.
The grounds of the Śrāvakas and the Pratyekabuddhas
Do provoke great terror in him.

AV "If the bodhisattva were confronted with the prospect of abiding in the hell-realms amidst their countless hundreds of thousands of sufferings, he would not find this more frightening than the prospect of falling down onto the grounds of the Śrāvaka disciples and Pratyekabuddhas."

027 – Whereas Hells Don't Block Buddhahood, Two Vehicles' Grounds Do

It is not the case that falling into the hell realms
Would create an ultimate obstacle to bodhi.
If one fell onto the grounds of the Śrāvakas or Pratyekabuddhas,
That would create an ultimate obstacle.

AV Although falling into the hells does create an obstacle, it is only temporary. Entering the paths of the Two Vehicles, however, does create a permanent obstacle making the bodhi of a buddha entirely inaccessible. Hence the bodhisattva would be more frightened at this latter possibility than by the prospect of falling into the hells.

TN The point at which, having entered a Two-Vehicles' path, one can no longer turn back from the nirvāṇa of the arhat or pratyeka-buddha is called "the right and fixed position" (*samyaktva niyāma*), a stage on the individual-liberation path synonymous with attainment of the path of seeing, a stage from which one not already invested with the confirmed resolve to achieve buddhahood cannot readily switch over to cultivation of the bodhisattva vehicle path to complete buddhahood. Nāgārjuna points out elsewhere in this treatise that the arhats given predictions of buddhahood (in the *Lotus Sutra*) were special cases, this most likely because they were bodhisattvas manifesting in the guise of arhats. Having noted this, bodhisattva practitioners not of that special class should indeed fear the prospect of falling away from Mahāyāna *bodhicitta* as being infinitely more hazardous than the prospect of falling into the hells.

028 – The Bodhisattva Should Fear Two-Vehicles Grounds Like the Gallows

Just as is said of one who loves long life
That he is frightened at the prospect of being beheaded,
So too the grounds of the Śrāvakas and Pratyekabuddhas
Should provoke in one this very sort of fear.

AV Bhikshu Vaśitva attributes this teaching to the Buddha himself and then introduces the following *śloka* as facilitating understanding of the means for developing the unproduced-dharmas patience.

---

029 – The Tetralemma-Transcending Contemplation of Dharmas

As for "not produced and not destroyed,"
And "neither unproduced nor undestroyed,"
One denies assertions of "both" and "neither."
So too in cases involving "emptiness" and "non-emptiness."

AV The commentator provides a tour of all tetralemma propositions, showing how all of them are refutable and none of them reflect reality.

TN The "tetralemma" is simply the four basic logical propositions: "X"; "not-X"; "both X and not-X"; and "neither X nor not-X." Even the most subtle logical formulations fall short in their attempts to describe ultimate reality, which is after all beyond the range of both mental conception and verbal description. Nāgārjuna states elsewhere (in the *Mahāprajñāpāramitā Upadeśa*) that ultimate reality is a great conflagration that cannot be touched by the "hands" of the tetralemma. Implicit in this is the recognition that ultimate truth is only approachable via the direct experience of the emptiness of all dharmas. This is in turn only possible through a non-conceptual awareness abandoning all mental discriminations developed through the combination of deep meditative stillness and wisdom-generating contemplation (*śamatha-vipaśyanā*).

---

030 – Unshakable Contemplation in the Unproduced-Dharmas Patience

No matter which "existent" dharma one encounters,
One persists therein in the contemplation, remaining unmoving.
That is the "unproduced-dharmas patience."
It is based on the severance of all mental discriminations.

AV The bodhisattva contemplates phenomena in accordance with reality, thus abandoning the view that any dharma possesses any intrinsic existence of its own. Dharmas, being mere aggregations of conditions, "exist" only in the manner of a bundled sheaf of reeds, a magical conjuration, or a mere dream. This realization, synonymous with the "unproduced-dharmas patience," makes one's reality-based contemplation of dharmas unshakably solid and allows one to abide on the "unmoving" bodhisattva ground (*acala bhūmi*).

---

031 – The Prediction and Irreversibility Come with Unproduced-Dharmas Patience

Once one gains this patience,
One immediately receives the prediction:
"You will definitely become a buddha."
It is then that one achieves "irreversibility."

AV Immediately on gaining unproduced-dharmas patience, all buddhas appear and bestow a specific prediction of buddhahood. This constitutes "irreversibility."

Next *śloka* is then introduced via this question: Why are the first seven stages of bodhisattvas, all certainly progressing toward *saṃbodhi*, not recognized as "irreversible"? Why is only this eighth-stage bodhisattva declared to be "irreversible"?

---

032 – Only This "Stage of Immovability" Guarantees Definite "Irreversibility"

Those bodhisattvas already dwelling at "the stage of immovability"
Have gained irreversible wisdom cognizing all dharmas' reality.
As their wisdom cannot be turned back by Two-vehicles adherents,
It is only at this point that they are designated as "irreversible."

AV The wisdom referred to here in fact alludes to all of the five world-transcendent root faculties consisting of faith, [vigor, mindfulness, concentration, and wisdom]. Although bodhisattvas beneath this stage can be caused to turn back and retreat from their aspiration to gain buddhahood, not so with these eighth-stage "definitely irreversible" bodhisattvas.

Regarding the "predictions of buddhahood" mentioned in the previous *śloka*, there are basically four kinds (which Bhikshu Vaśitva discusses):

1) Predictions bestowed prior to generating *bodhicitta*;
2) Predictions bestowed upon generating *bodhicitta*;
3) "Concealed" predictions; and
4) "Direct presence" predictions wherein the Buddhas bestow the prediction of buddhahood in the direct presence of the recipient. This is the type bestowed on this eighth-stage bodhisattva when he gains unproduced-dharmas patience and abides on the "unmoving" eighth bodhisattva stage characterized by ultimate irreversibility.

There is in addition a fifth category of "secretly-intentioned and specially-spoken" predictions such as figure in the *Lotus Sutra* wherein the Buddha apparently bestowed predictions on beings manifesting as arhats. The real meaning behind such predictions is known only to the Buddhas.

---

033 – No Negligence Can Be Indulged Prior to the "Direct Presence" Ground

Until the bodhisattva has gained
The solid samādhis
On the ground of all Buddhas' "direct presence,"
He should not allow any negligence to arise.

AV Until these samādhis are gained, the bodhisattva is still vulnerable to falling into the wretched destinies and is still vulnerable to being reborn in "the eight difficulties."

As for "samādhi," this refers to abiding in a uniformly even [and profoundly deep] mind state [achieved through the practice of meditation]. More specifically, this refers to three types of samādhis:

1)   Those involving mental transformation of form-based objective conditions.

2)   Those involving mental transformation of Dharma-related objective conditions.

3)   Those involving no mental transformation of any objective conditions whatsoever.

The first is the meditative terrain accessible to the newly-resolved bodhisattva. The second is that achievable by those who have entered the bodhisattva practices. The third is the domain of the bodhisattva who has realized the unproduced-dharmas patience.

TN The ground of "direct presence" (*abhimukha-bhūmi*) is the sixth of the ten bodhisattva grounds. The "eight difficulties" refers to eight terribly unfortunate rebirth circumstances wherein one has little hope of being able to cultivate the Path. This refers to the following types of unfortunate rebirth:

1)   In the hell realms.
2)   In the hungry-ghost realms.
3)   In the animal realms.
4)   On the most blissful continent.
5)   In the long-life heavens.
6)   In the condition of being deaf, mute, or blind.
7)   Possessing worldliness-obsessed eloquence and intelligence.
8)   At a time either before or after a buddha's Dharma reign.

034 – Samādhis Are a Bodhisattva's Father, Compassion and Patience Are Mother

The solid samādhis
On the ground of all Buddhas' "direct presence"
Serve for the bodhisattva as his father,
Whereas the great compassion and patiences serve as his mother.

AV Because these samādhis focus on the qualities of the Buddhas and the Bodhisattvas, they are said to serve as the father of the bodhisattva.

Because the great compassion prevents weariness with cyclic existence and prevents falling over the precipice down to the motivation-level of individual-liberation paths, it is said to serve as the mother of the bodhisattva.

Because the patiences prevent disgust with cyclic existence and the evil beings therein, it too is said to serve as the mother of the bodhisattvas.

035 – Wisdom as Mother and Means as Father is Due to Giving Birth and Support

As for the perfection of wisdom being his mother
And skillful means being his father,
It is because the one gives him birth and the other supports him
That they are said to be the bodhisattva's father and mother.

AV This is an additional verse reflecting a different approach to explaining the spiritual parentage of the bodhisattva. The dharmas of the bodhisattva are born forth from the perfection of wisdom, hence its designation as the bodhisattva's mother. Skillful means sustain the bodhisattva on the Path, preventing him from falling down a treacherous precipice onto the grounds of the Śrāvaka disciples and the Pratyekabuddhas. Hence it may be said to be the bodhisattva's father.

036 – Only Merit Greater Than a Hundred Sumerus Would Be Adequate for Bodhi

With but a lesser accumulation of merit
One remains unable to realize bodhi.
Only by collecting merit more massive than a hundred Sumerus
Can one succeed in achieving that realization.

AV "Bodhi" refers to the realization of a level of wisdom corresponding in its extensiveness to omniscience. Such knowledge is as infinitely vast as space itself and as such, it requires an accumulation of merit greater than the mass of a hundred Mt. Sumerus for its realization.

―――――

TN Bhikshu Vaśitva introduces the next *śloka* with a challenger's question insisting that, were this assertion actually true, given the incredible quantity of requisite merit, not even one single person would ever become capable of realizing bodhi. The methods for accumulating such a staggeringly great measure of merit are then explained in the *ślokas* which follow.

---

037 – Through Skillful Means, a Minor Deed Generates Great Merit

Although one may perform but a minor meritorious deed,
Even in this, one possesses a skillful means:
Taking the sphere of "all beings" as the object,
One should generate a mental transformation of the conditions.

AV By using the skillful means of mentally dedicating the merit from even a minor good deed to the goal of bringing about the bodhi of all beings, the bodhisattva is able to make that small amount of merit infinite in scope. Thus, even though the enlightenment he wishes to achieve is so vast, he will still be enabled by this skillful means to generate the massive amount of merit required for realization of buddhahood.

---

038 – How Could One Measure the Merit of Such Universally-Dedicated Deeds?

Where one reflects: "May whatever actions I undertake
Always be done for the welfare of beings,"
Who could measure the merit of he
Whose mental actions are of this sort?

AV Who aside from the Buddhas could be able to gauge the merit of anyone dedicating the merit from his own good deeds to the liberation of all beings, doing so through perfection of the great compassion and through the implementation of excellent skillful means? Bhikshu Vaśitva introduces the next *śloka* with a question: "How might this merit become even more incalculably vast?"

039 – When Free of Attachments, When Not Coveting Even the Heavens—

Where one isn't constrained by fondness for relatives, retinue,
Body, life, or wealth,
Where one isn't held back by desiring pleasure in Iśvara's heavens,
Brahma-world heavens, or any other heavens,

040 – Not Coveting Nirvāṇa, Yet Caring for Others, Who Could Gauge Such Merit?

Where one isn't constrained even by coveting nirvāṇa,
Where one's actions are done for the sake of other beings,
And where in all this, one thinks only of the welfare of beings,
Who then could measure the vastness of his merit?

AV The bodhisattva thinks, "How shall I be able to influence these beings, these child-like common people blinded by the cataracts of ignorance? How shall I be able to cause them to gain liberation from the prison of the three realms so that they become established in the constant bliss of nirvāṇa's city of fearlessness?"

When this bodhisattva carries out these endeavors bestowing benefit and happiness, acting with such kindness toward beings, who could measure the extent of his merit?

———

TN The "three realms" (proceeding from coarsest to most refined) are: the desire realm, the form realm, and the formless realm. They correspond to thirty-one planes of cyclic existence, as follows:

The "desire realm" is comprised of the five lowest levels of rebirth consisting of the hells, animals, ghost realms (*preta*), humans, the demi-gods or "titans" (*asura*); and the six coarsest levels of celestial rebirth known as "the six desire heavens." (The lowest three desire-realm rebirth destinies consisting of hells, animals, and ghost realms comprise what are referred to as "the three wretched destinies" (*durgati*).)

The "form realm" is comprised of sixteen levels of intermediate celestial rebirth corresponding to the meditation states encountered in the four dhyānas.

The "formless realm" is comprised of the four most refined levels of celestial rebirth corresponding to the four formless meditation states.

041 – Rescuing and Protecting the Vulnerable, Who Could Measure Such Merit?

When for those of the world without refuge or protection,
He rescues and protects them from their bitter afflictions—
When he raises forth such thoughts and actions as these,
Who could possibly measure his merit?

AV The bodhisattva, instigated by the great compassion, reflects thus: "Beings have no one to rescue or protect them. They wander throughout the six rebirth destinies, plunging into the fires of the three types of suffering. Having no place of refuge, they chase about hither and thither. In all of their physical and mental sicknesses, they are constantly beset by bitter afflictions. I shall be a refuge for them, rescuing them from physical and mental sufferings."

TN The "six rebirth destinies" cited by Bhikshu Vaśitva are: celestials, demigods (*asura*), humans, animals, ghosts (*preta*), hells (*niraya*).

The "three types of suffering" are:

1) The suffering of suffering (*duḥkha-duḥkhatā*).

2) The suffering inherent in conditioned existence, i.e. that associated with the karmic formative factors (*saṃskāra-duḥkhatā*).

3) The suffering wrought by change, i.e. through deterioration of states not recognized as subject to suffering (*pariṇāma-duḥkhatā*).

042 – So It Is in a Moment Aligned with Wisdom. If Longer, Who Could Gauge It?

It would be so even in according with the perfection of wisdom
For only the moment of tugging forth a stream of cow's milk.
If one acted thus for a month or for many more months,
Who could possibly measure his merit?

AV This prajñāpāramitā is able to give birth to all buddhas and bodhisattvas and perfect all dharmas of buddhas and bodhisattvas. Hence the immense merit from even a moment's alignment therewith. Where it continues on, who could possibly measure his accumulation of merit?

043 – Recitation and Teaching of Profound Sutras Creates Massive Merit

Where one recites to himself or teaches to others
Those profound sutras praised by the Buddhas—
Also, where one interprets and explains them for others—
These are the bases of an accumulation of merit.

AV "Profound sutras" are those teaching emptiness, transcendence of the world, and causality. The Dharma is synonymous with the body of the Tathāgata, hence where one recites, teaches, or explains these profound sutras out of a selfless motivation to keep the Tathāgata's body from disappearing from the world, the merit generated thereby is so vast as to defy measurement.

---

044 – Through Inspiring Bodhi Resolve, Superior Merit and Eighth Stage Are Assured

Through influencing countless beings
To generate the bodhi resolve,
One's treasury of merit increases yet more
And one becomes bound to gain "the ground of immovability."

AV This bodhisattva, using the four means of attraction, first draws in beings and then, when they are ready, teaches them in a manner inspiring them to seek the highest enlightenment.

It is in the nature of this bodhisattva's ability to cause others to resolve on enlightenment that it inevitably creates for him an inexhaustible reserve of merit, inevitably causes his own unshakable resolve to be renewed in life after life, and inevitably causes him to eventually reach "the ground of immovability," [the eighth of the ten bodhisattva grounds].

---

045 – Turning the Dharma Wheel and Stilling Heterodoxies Makes a Merit Treasury

Where one follows in turning what the Buddha turned,
The wheel of the supreme Dharma,
Thus clearing away all of the "noxious thorns,"
This creates the bodhisattva's treasury of merit.

AV One follows the example of the Buddha in turning the wheel of Dharma, particularly in three ways directly related to profound sutras teaching emptiness:

1) One preserves these sutras, preventing their disappearance.

2) One provides analytic explanations of these teachings for those with the capacity to fathom and retain their import.

3) One cultivates the Path in accordance with their Dharma.

Outside of the Dharma communities, "noxious thorns" is a reference to the erroneous views held by non-Buddhists and to the actions of demons and denizens of the desire realm's sovereign independence heavens.

Within the Dharma communities, "noxious thorns" refers to unorthodox members of the four-fold assembly promoting non-Dharma as Dharma, promoting wrong behavior as consistent with the moral codes, and promoting teachings not taught by the Guru to have been taught by the Guru. Through means consistent with Dharma (as through debate and insistence on adherence to the moral codes), such individuals should be vanquished so that their arrogance is shattered, their views are demolished, and right Dharma is allowed to flourish.

These actions all serve as means for the bodhisattva to establish a treasury of merit.

---

046 – Where One Is Willing to Suffer the Hells for Beings, Bodhi Is at Hand

Where, to benefit beings and make them happy,
One would endure even the sufferings of the great hells,
How much the more the other lesser sufferings,
It is as if bodhi lay in the palm of one's own right hand.

AV This refers to the bodhisattva who dons the armor [of patience], works to bring benefit and happiness to beings, generates intensely diligent resolve, and is willing to suffer for eons in the great *avīci* hells to liberate beings. One should realize that, for a bodhisattva of this sort, it is as if bodhi already lay in the palm of his hand.

---

047 – Where Actions Are Selfless, Altruistic, and Compassionate, Bodhi Is at Hand

Where whatever one does, it is not for one's self,
But solely to benefit beings and make them happy—
Because this all arises from the great compassion,
It is as if bodhi lay in the palm of one's own right hand.

AV The bodhisattva's actions all arise from compassion, are selflessly motivated, and are intended to bring benefit, happiness, and nirvāṇa to beings. For such compassionate beings, it is as if bodhi has already arrived in the palm of the hand.

---

048 – Where Wisdom, Vigor, and Giving Are Transcendent, Bodhi Is at Hand

Where wisdom is such that one abandons frivolous discourse,
Where vigor is such that one abandons indolence,
And where giving is such that one abandons miserliness,
It is as if bodhi lay in the palm of one's own right hand.

AV These perfections are described here in reference to those possessing the wisdom associated with that patience in which no phenomenon's intrinsic existence is deemed apprehensible.

Such wisdom realizes the singular character of the Path, such vigor refuses to set aside the yoke [of the bodhisattva practices], and such giving has gotten rid of all covetousness.

———

TN This *śloka* and the next collectively describe all six perfections as they occur in fully-developed bodhisattva practice.

---

049 – Where Meditation, Moral Virtue, and Patience Are Perfected, Bodhi Is at Hand

Where meditation is such that one is free of reliances or ideation,
Where morality is such that its practice is perfect and unmixed,
And where patience is such that one realizes non-production,
It is as if bodhi lay in the palm of one's own right hand.

AV This bodhisattva's meditation doesn't rely on anything in the three realms, is quiescently still, and is devoid of any contemplative ideation. His observance of *śīla* is perfect, free of defilements, dedicated to bodhi and invulnerable to deterioration. He has so well perfected prajñāpāramitā that he abides in the unproduced-dharmas patience even in the midst of dharmas produced through the conjunction of conditions.

Due to the supremacy of the foundations, such bodhisattvas become non-retreating in their practice.

The above discussion describes the seasoned bodhisattva. But the question now arises: How should the beginning bodhisattva proceed in accumulating the merit essential for bodhi?

---

050 – One Confesses All Bad Deeds in the Presence of All Buddhas

In the abodes of all who have gained the right enlightenment,
Now abiding throughout the ten directions,
I appear there in the presence of them all,
And completely lay forth all my unwholesome deeds.

AV One reflects: "I go before all buddhas everywhere and confess all of my past and present-life karmic transgressions, including all those done by others at my behest, including all those not done by me but nonetheless joyfully approved of by me, including all those arising through desire, hatefulness, or delusion, and including all those committed through body, mouth, or mind. I confess them all, conceal none, and vow to cease them forever."

---

051 – One Entreats the Buddhas to Turn the Dharma Wheel

Where there are buddhas who have realized bodhi
In those realms throughout the ten directions,
But they have not yet proclaimed the Dharma,
I entreat them to turn the Dharma wheel.

AV This is done out of pity for beings in the world, is done for the sake of the members of the Great Assembly, and is done with the wish that benefit and happiness will be bestowed on both gods and men.

---

052 – One Beseeches the Buddhas to Remain in the World

Wherever there are those possessing the right enlightenment
Abiding in the present era in the ten directions' realms,
But now on the verge of relinquishing their lives and actions,
I bow down my head in reverence, beseeching them to remain.

AV One reflects: "Wherever there are buddhas anywhere in the ten directions who have already gained the right enlightenment, turned the Dharma wheel, established right Dharma, instructed beings, and liberated beings—when they are on the verge of relinquishing their lives and their Dharma activities in favor of the final nirvāṇa, I shall go there and bow down my head in reverence, beseeching them to remain for a long time, benefiting and bringing happiness to the multitudes."

---

053 – All Merit Created by Beings Through Giving on Through to Meditation—

Wherever there may be any beings
Who, by acts of body, mouth, or mind,
Have created any merit through giving, moral virtue,
And so forth, including through cultivation of meditation—

---

054 – Whether Created by Āryas or Common People, I Rejoice in It All

No matter whether they be āryas or common persons—
And no matter whether its creation is past, present, or future—
I am moved to rejoice
In all of that accumulated merit.

AV One reflects: "I rejoice in all merit created by any being in the past, present, or future, no matter whether via body, mouth, or mind, and no matter whether that being be an ārya or a common person." Only such entirely comprehensive rejoicing should be regarded as [genuine] rejoicing.

TN Two topics deserve attention here:

1) It is clear from the wording and syntax of the *śloka* phrases I translate as "...through giving, moral virtue, / And so forth, including through cultivation of meditation—" that Nāgārjuna is referring to the "three bases of meritorious activity" (*puṇya-kriyā-vastu*) encountered in both the Theravada and Mahāyāna canons. Specifically, they are giving, moral virtue, and meditation (*dāna, śīla, bhāvanā*).

2) The important Mahāyāna concept I translate here as "rejoicing in the creation of merit" (*puṇya-anumodana*) may seem opaque until one digests all implications of the idea. First, one's deep appreciation and rejoicing extends to include all forms of goodness which ever have been or ever will be done, from the least significant to the most sublime, and from that done by the lowest creatures on up to that done by the Mahāsattvas and the Buddhas.

Finally, this "accordant rejoicing" has the additional secondary implication that not only does one feel so deeply appreciative of others' meritorious actions that one feels complete approval and delight in it, but one also feels inspired to follow along in doing such good deeds oneself.

---

055 – I Dedicate All Merit to All Beings That They Might Realize Bodhi

If all of the merit I have created
Could be formed into a single ball,
I would bestow it on all beings through dedicating it
To causing them to gain the right enlightenment.

AV I dedicate all merit to bodhi with the intention of causing all beings to realize the highest enlightenment, including in this dedication all merit ever created by me across the course of cyclic existence in my interactions with the Three Jewels and with other persons, including even all merit created from generosity to animals, from taking the Three Refuges, from repentance of transgressions, from requesting the Buddhas to turn the Dharma wheel, from beseeching the Buddhas to remain in the world, and from rejoicing in the merit created by others.

---

056 – To Repent, Entreat, Beseech, Rejoice, and Dedicate Accords with Buddhas' Acts

As for these actions I undertake in repenting transgressions,
In entreating and beseeching, in rejoicing in others' merit,
And so on, including in dedicating all merit to realizing bodhi—
One should realize they accord with all buddhas' own practices.

AV Repentance of transgressions, entreating buddhas to turn the Dharma wheel, beseeching buddhas to stay in the world, rejoicing in others' good deeds, and dedicating one's merit to the goal that oneself and all beings will realize the highest enlightenment— these actions are precisely those undertaken by all buddhas of the past, present, and future while still on the Bodhisattva Path. Consequently one now takes up these very same practices as well.

---

057 – To Repent, Entreat, Beseech, Rejoice, and Dedicate Accords with Their Teachings

These acts of confession and repentance of my bad karmic deeds,
Of entreating the Buddhas, of rejoicing in others' merit,
And so on, including dedicating all merit to realizing bodhi—
These all accord with teachings set forth by the Victorious One.

AV Because all of these acts conform to the practices coursed in by all of the Buddhas themselves and because they accord with the teachings as presented by the Buddha himself, one now adopts just such practices oneself.

---

058 – Thrice Daily, Thrice Nightly, Kneeling with Shoulder Bared, Palms Together

Kneeling down with the right knee touching the ground
And the upper robe arranged to bare one shoulder,
Three times each day and three times each night,
Press the palms together and proceed in this manner.

AV With clean body and robes and freshly-washed hands and feet, arrange the robe neatly with the right shoulder bared. Kneel with the right knee touching the ground and palms pressed together. Abandon discursive thought and focus the mind.

Then, having done this before a buddha stupa, buddha image, or visualized image of the Buddha, proceed to perform the above-described acts [of repentance and so forth]. One engages in this practice three times each day and three times each night.

___

TN Even though Ārya Nāgārjuna's instructions happen to specifically reference a monastic's robes in the performance of this practice, there would be no reason to infer that it is not equally recommended as an essential practice for the laity as well. The details regarding arrangement of robes are only intended to indicate the need to maintain an attitude of deep sincerity, reverence, and focus as one carries out this daily practice.

___

059 – Merit From But a Single Instance of This Would Be Incalculably Immense

The merit created in even a single instance of doing this,
If manifest in material form, would be so immense
That even a Ganges' sands of great chiliocosms
Would still be unable to contain it.

___

AV The Buddha described the accumulation of merit from this sort of practice in these terms. Thus, although one might be only a beginning bodhisattva, due to the power inherent in such an act of merit dedication, one still creates a huge measure of merit. Consequently, because one draws upon such an accumulation of merit, one gradually becomes able with the assistance of such practices to achieve the realization of bodhi.

___

060 – Revere and Cherish Minor Bodhisattvas As One Respects Guru and Parents

Having brought forth the initial resolve,
In relations with minor bodhisattvas,
One should bring forth for them veneration and cherishing
Comparable to that felt for the Guru and parents.

___

AV Having thus taken those other initial-resolve bodhisattvas as the first object of concern, these beginning bodhisattvas should then also raise forth just such thoughts of ultimate veneration and cherishing respectfulness toward all other bodhisattvas as well

Were one to act in a manner varying from this, one's very own person could become destined for destruction along with all of one's previously-established roots of goodness. This is just as stated in the scriptures by the Bhagavān himself when he stated, "I see no other single dharma so effective in obstructing a bodhisattva and completely destroying all of his roots of goodness as the act of generating hateful thoughts toward other bodhisattvas."

TN Nāgārjuna's rationale for focusing on beginning bodhisattvas as the primary object of concern in this *śloka* probably has to do with the fact that it would be easiest for another novice bodhisattva's critical eye to find fault with them, thus most easily stumbling thereby into an unwitting, but nonetheless "fatal" karmic mistake.

---

061 – Don't Discuss a Bodhisattva's Faults; Utter Only Truth-Based Praise

Although a bodhisattva may have committed transgressions,
One should still not speak about them,
How much the less so where there is no truth to the matter.
One should utter praises only where they are grounded in truth.

AV If one becomes involved in creating a bad reputation for a Mahāyāna practitioner by revealing his karmic transgressions to others, one thereby destroys one's own accumulated good karma and makes it personally impossible to develop the practice of pure dharmas. The care one must adopt in such matters is comparable to that observed in avoiding even mentioning the crimes of a king.

A story from the Sutras describes a monk erring in this regard as having suffered the karmic retribution of seventy kalpas in the hells followed by sixty thousand lifetimes of poverty, blindness, muteness, and horrible physical appearance.

Therefore, to protect one's own roots of karmic goodness, one's own karmic future, and the ability of others to develop faith in the Mahāyāna, one must refrain from spreading rumors about those who have taken up the Bodhisattva Path. Then again, one should only proclaim the good qualities of such individuals where one knows such statements are true.

---

062 – To Prevent Retreat from Bodhi, Show the Way, Promote Vigor, Inspire Delight

Where someone has vowed to become a buddha
And one wishes to prevent his retreat from that resolve,
Reveal the way with such clarity he brims with intense vigor,
And cause him to be filled with delight.

AV Where someone who has already vowed to become a buddha is tempted to adopt *śrāvaka*-disciple practices and pursue rapid realization of that path's nirvāṇa, use many and varied analogies to make the qualities of buddhahood manifestly clear to him. Through skillful descriptions, cause him to be fired with vigor. To promote swift success, describe the qualities attending the right enlightenment, including the spiritual powers, this to inspire delight in practice. These are appropriate means for preventing retreat from bodhisattva resolve.

---

063 – Don't Claim Buddhas Didn't Utter the Profound Sutras; Retribution is Severe

Where one hasn't yet understood extremely profound scriptures,
One must not claim they were not spoken by a buddha.
If one makes statements of this sort,
One suffers the most bitter and horrible of karmic retributions.

AV "Extremely profound scriptures," refers to teachings on emptiness, signlessness, and wishlessness, teachings refuting extreme views such as annihilationism and eternalism, teachings demolishing the inherent existence of self, others, beings, or a life, and teachings revealing a buddha's powers and qualities.

If, based on one's own delusions, one slanders scriptures spoken by buddhas, the karmic retribution is bound to be horrible.

---

064 – Not Even the "Non-intermittent Offenses" Can Compare to These Two Offenses

If the karmic offenses generating "non-intermittent" retributions
Were all put together to form a single ball
And were compared to one formed from the above two offenses,
They would not amount to even the smallest fraction thereof.

AV In the *Irreversible Wheel Sutra*, the Buddha compares these types of karmic offenses (per the following paraphrase):

Suppose one took all of the bad karma associated with all karmic transgressions generating the "non-intermittent" (*avīci* hell) retributions and formed them together into a single ball. Then suppose one compared the size of that ball with one formed to represent the mass of bad karma arising from just two karmic offenses:

1) Claiming the profound sutras weren't spoken by buddhas.
2) Causing someone already resolved on gaining buddhahood to retreat from that resolve.

Having made that comparison, we would find that the former would not equal even a tiny fraction of the latter.

Due to the especially potent negative character of these karmic offenses and due to the necessity to guard one's own person and one's roots of karmic goodness, one must not commit either of these two types of karmic offenses.

———

TN Two topics require clarification here: a) "non-intermittent retribution"; and b) reconciliation of the "two offenses" specifically noted by Nāgārjuna in his own *śloka* text with the two offenses described in Bhikshu Vaśitva's sutra citation.

The "five non-intermittent retributions" associated with the most extremely grave karmic offenses are:

1) No intervening rebirths prior to direct descent into the hells.

2) Non-intermittent continuity of hell punishments.

3) Non-intermittency of that period of time wherein punishments are undergone.

4) Non-intermittency of lifespan during karmic punishments (i.e. no temporary "escapes" via death).

5) Non-intermittency of the space occupied by one's body as it undergoes karmic punishments. (i.e., whatever the size of the particular hell, one's body is of commensurate size, undergoing excruciating tortures on every square inch of its entire expanse.

On the matter of reconciling the "two offenses" specifically noted by Nāgārjuna in his own *śloka* text with the two offenses described in Bhikshu Vaśitva's sutra citation, first note that Nāgārjuna refers directly to:

a) "Although a bodhisattva may have committed transgressions, one should still not speak about them, how much the less so where there is no truth to the matter."

b) "Where one hasn't yet understood extremely profound scriptures, one must not claim they were not spoken by a buddha."

Bhikshu Vaśitva on the other hand seems to agree completely on the second ("claiming profound sutras weren't spoken by buddhas"), while seeming to vary somewhat on the first, implying via the sutra citation that this refers to "Causing someone already resolved on bodhi to retreat from that resolve."

A closer look at Nāgārjuna's treatise text reveals that any apparent difference here is insubstantial and that the two discussions may be reconciled as follows:

"Causing someone already resolved on bodhi to retreat from that resolve" is more-or-less "implicit" in each of Nāgārjuna's immediately preceding four *ślokas*, this because, were we to fail at the concerns in any of the four *ślokas*, it could very likely cause someone formerly resolved on buddhahood to abandon the entire endeavor. The logic is as follows:

1) Where one fails to be kind and respectful toward a newly-resolved bodhisattva, we may discourage him, thus causing him to retreat from his resolve (*śloka* 60).

2) Where one either broadcasts the karmic errors or falsely claims the virtues of followers of the Bodhisattva Path, this may cause one formerly resolved on buddhahood to retreat from his resolve (*śloka* 61).

3) Where we fail to assist discouraged practitioners with inspiring teachings about the nature of the Bodhisattva Path and the unique qualities of buddhas, this may cause one formerly resolved on buddhahood to retreat from his resolve (*śloka* 62).

4) Where we claim profound sutras describing the Bodhisattva Path weren't spoken by buddhas, this too may cause one formerly resolved on buddhahood to retreat from his resolve (*śloka* 63).

Although one easily appreciates the validity of Bhikshu Vaśitva's interpretation and the inherent identity of the principles discussed in both texts, I suspect Ārya Nāgārjuna deliberately stressed the two offenses so clearly articulated in his own treatise text and that these two were the ones he intended to reference in *śloka* 63.

---

065 – One Should Cultivate the Three Gates to Liberation

One should skillfully cultivate
The three gates to liberation:
The first is emptiness, the next is signlessness,
And the third is wishlessness.

AV Because the bodhisattva practices the perfection of wisdom, he should cultivate these three gates to liberation. One employs "emptiness" to refute views, employs "signlessness" to eliminate any tendency to seize on mental discriminations or manipulations., and employs "wishlessness" to transcend all three realms of existence.

TN "The three gates to liberation," also known as "the three samādhis," are discussed at great length by Ārya Nāgārjuna in his *Mahāprajñāparamitā Upadeśa*. For a complete translation, see the appropriate chapter in my forthcoming *Nāgārjuna on Emptiness*.

066 – Dharmas Are "Empty" of Inherent Existence, Hence Signless, Hence Wishless

Because they have no self-existent nature, phenomena are empty.
If already empty, how could one establish any characteristic signs?
Since all characteristic signs are themselves in a state of cessation,
What could there be in them that the wise might wish for?

AV Because dharmas are produced from a mere conjunction of conditions, they have no inherent nature of their own and hence are described as "empty" of inherent existence.

Because dharmas are empty of inherent existence, the mind refrains from imputing any particular qualities to them. Hence we speak of their being "signless."

In the absence of any intrinsic qualities, there is no basis for the mind's finding in dharmas anything worthy of generating aspirations about them. Hence we speak of their being "wishless."

TN The stock translation "wishlessness" (*apraṇihita*) may seem mildly confusing at first glance. It simply means that, once one realizes the true character of any and all phenomena, i.e. that they are devoid of any genuine intrinsic nature of their own, one realizes that they are devoid of any genuine means through which to provoke the mind into aspirations on their behalf. In short, "emptiness" and "signlessness" provoke the question to which one immediately realizes there is no sensible answer: "If there's no *there* to be found there, why would you want to go there?"

Understanding of emptiness, signlessness, and wishlessness may be facilitated by contemplating dharmas from several standpoints: a) as mere temporary conjunctions of subsidiary conditions (per Bhikshu Vaśitva); b) as involving only "names" with no genuinely-existent substrates; and c) as merely micro-momentary products of a process of serial chronological production, this last standpoint being best aided through meditation on "the twelve links of conditioned co-production" (*pratītya-samutpāda*).

067 – As These Tend Toward Nirvāṇa, Focus on the Causes Leading to Buddhahood

When cultivating the mindful awareness of these,
One draws close to those paths leading into nirvāṇa.
Do not bear in mind anything not resulting in a buddha's body
And, in that matter, one must not allow any negligence.

AV When one cultivates these three gates to liberation, because one's level of realization leads one close to entering nirvāṇa, one must exert control through artful use of skillful means to avoid it.

TN The point in this *śloka* is that, in cultivating the three gates to liberation, if one fails to remain focused on the Mahāyāna quest for the utmost, right, and perfect enlightenment of a buddha, one will proceed on through these three gates right into the nirvāṇa realized by the arhat or pratyekabuddha with the tragic result that one forever loses the Bodhisattva Path.

One can only become a buddha through completing the cultivation of the bodhisattva's six perfections and myriad practices. It is because there is absolutely no room for deviation in aiming one's determination accordingly that Nāgārjuna finishes the *śloka* with two imperative warnings, lest we lose the Bodhisattva Path:

1) "Do not bear in mind anything not resulting in a buddha's body."
2) "And, in that matter, one must not allow any negligence."

---

068 – Resolve to Abstain from Nirvāṇa; Rather Ripen the Perfection of Wisdom

"In this matter of nirvāṇa,
I must not immediately invoke its realization."
One should initiate this sort of resolve,
For one must succeed in ripening the perfection of wisdom.

AV One generates just this sort of thought: "I shall bring about the benefit and liberation of all beings. Although I shall cultivate the three gates to liberation, it shall be with the exclusive aim of ripening my practice of the perfection of wisdom. Hence I must refrain from opting for the ultimate realization of emptiness, signlessness, wishlessness, and nirvāṇa."

---

069 – The Great Bodhisattva Is Like the Skillful Archer Keeping His Arrows Aloft

Just as an archer might shoot his arrows upwards,
Causing each in succession to strike the one before,
Each holding up the other so none are allowed to fall—
Just so it is with the great bodhisattva.

AV This is analogous to a hypothetical instance wherein a well-trained archer might release his arrows into the sky in succession, continuously releasing them so that each succeeding arrow supports the one before and none are allowed to fall.

---

070 – Even in Realizing Emptiness, the Mind's Arrows Never Fall to Nirvāṇa's Ground

Into the emptiness of the gates to liberation,
He skillfully releases the arrows of the mind.
Through artful skillful means, arrows are continuously held aloft,
So none are allowed to fall back down into nirvāṇa.

AV The bodhisattva, like a great archer, releases arrows of mind into the emptiness of the three gates, also using skillful means arrows of compassion. He continues to release them into the emptiness of the three realms, causing them to remain suspended and hence unable to fall down into the city of nirvāṇa.

---

071 – One Makes the Altruistic Vow and Thenceforth Accords Therewith

"I shall not forsake beings,
But rather shall continue on for the sake of benefiting beings."
One first initiates this very sort of intention,
And thenceforth ensures that his practice corresponds thereto.

AV The bodhisattva reflects: "Through ripening my cultivation of the three gates to liberation, I could seize nirvāṇa as if it already lay in my hand. However, because common people are as helpless as nursing infants, they cannot make their own way to the city of nirvāṇa. Hence it is not right that I abandon them and enter nirvāṇa alone. Therefore, I'll avail myself of vigor and remain to benefit beings whilst also facilitating their future nirvāṇa."

First, one makes this resolve. Then, one ensures that one's subsequent actions accord with it. Were one to fail in this, practice of the three gates to liberation would instead lead to the solitary nirvāṇa of *śrāvakas* and pratyekabuddhas, this because such practice would not be guided by skillful means.

---

072 – Beings Abide in Attachment, Cherishing Inverted Views Caused by Delusion

There are beings who have become inured to attachment
Throughout time's long night and in present actions as well.
Their coursing in inverted views regarding characteristic signs
Is in every case due to confusion wrought by delusion.

AV Throughout cyclic existence, beings are attached through delusion to the four inverted views, imagining permanence, bliss, purity, and self where none of those can be found. Among the aggregates, sense realms, and sense bases, falsely reckon the existence of a self, appurtenances of a self, and supposedly apprehensible dharmas. Having carried on this way throughout time's long night, they continue on even now.

---

073 – Speak Dharma to Eliminate Attachments to Marks and Inverted Views

For those attached to marks and holding inverted views,
One explains the Dharma so such errors might be eliminated.
One first generates this very sort of resolve,
And thenceforth ensures that his practice corresponds thereto.

AV Due to delusion, beings impute existence of self and appurtenances of self, generate erroneous discriminations, seize upon their aspects, and develop the four inverted views.

One resolves: "I shall explain Dharma so they may eliminate such errors." One then proceeds accordingly, even while coursing in the three gates to liberation. Were one to stray from this approach while cultivating the three gates to liberation, one would become bound for direct entry into nirvāṇa.

---

074 – Bodhisattvas Help Beings, yet Perceive No Beings, and in This Are Inconceivable

The bodhisattva benefits beings
And yet does not perceive the existence of any being.
This in itself is the most difficult of all endeavors
And is such a rarity as to be inconceivable.

AV The bodhisattva's conceiving the idea of a "being" is in itself the most difficult and inconceivable endeavor, like painting in empty space. At the level of ultimate truth, "beings" don't even exist. The bodhisattva doesn't perceive beings as genuinely existent entities, yet he nonetheless proceeds with vigor in his attempts to bestow the ultimate benefit and happiness on beings. With the sole exception of the great compassion, where could there be any other endeavor so difficult as this?

---

075 – Though Realizing Definite Stage and Gates to Liberation, One Avoids Nirvāṇa

Although one may have entered "the right and definite position,"
And one's practice may accord with the gates to liberation,
Because one has not yet fulfilled one's original vows,
One refrains from proceeding to the realization of nirvāṇa.

AV We should reflect upon the situation of a bodhisattva who has reached "the right and definite position." This right and definite position is reached through reliance on thirty-two dharmas. One might well wonder whether, having already reached that stage, whether a bodhisattva coursing in the gates to liberation might not just go ahead and opt for the individual-liberation nirvāṇa rather than fulfil his original vows and proceed on to buddhahood. The Buddha declared in the sutras that this was impossible.

TN As for "the right and definite position" (*samyaktva-niyāma*), for the bodhisattva, this is typically held to coincide with the eighth bodhisattva ground, "the ground of unshakability" (*acala bhūmi*) wherein the bodhisattva has reached the stage of definite irreversibility in his path to buddhahood.

For a *śrāvaka* or pratyekabuddha, this "right and definite position" coincides with the Path of Seeing wherein the emptiness of all phenomena is perceived directly. From the standpoint of this treatise, once this position is reached, a *śrāvaka* practitioner is definitely bound for final nirvāṇa as an arhat and will definitely not be able to switch over to the Bodhisattva Path.

The rationale for Ārya Nāgārjuna's strong and repeated emphasis in this treatise on avoiding the nirvāṇa of the Śrāvaka Vehicle arhat is that, were the bodhisattva to allow himself to enter it through failing to maintain the skillful means and altruistic vow which would ordinarily prevent him from doing so, this would bring about an irreversible fall from the Bodhisattva Path from which someone aspiring to buddhahood cannot ever under any circumstances recover.

Even in spite of the teachings offered in the *Lotus Sutra* (which Nāgārjuna will discuss later), that is the position of this treatise. This entire issue is dealt with at much greater length in the ensuing *ślokas* of this treatise wherein Nāgārjuna offers the view that the *Lotus Sutra* circumstance was a special one specific to certain individuals which cannot be generalized to the general population of Buddhist practitioners who might otherwise feel that, even after arhatship, buddhahood might somehow be possible.

Now, even though Bhikshu Vaśitva cites a passage from the Sutras wherein the Buddha states that it is impossible that a bodhisattva who has already reached the right and definite position might stop short of complete buddhahood, opting instead for a solitary-liberation nirvāṇa, we should realize that this inability to stop short of buddhahood only becomes true once the "right and definite position" is reached. Up until that event has occurred coincident with the eighth bodhisattva ground, the bodhisattva is still vulnerable to being turned back to the individual-liberation nirvāṇa.

The "thirty-two dharmas of a bodhisattva" as set forth by Ārya Nāgārjuna's *Daśabhūmika Vibhāṣā* (T26.1521.93c–4a) are as follows:

1) With a profound mind, he seeks every form of happiness for all beings;
2) He is able to enter into the wisdom of the Buddhas;
3) Through his own investigations, he knows whether or not he is capable of becoming a buddha;
4) He does not course in detestation of others;
5) His mind intent on pursuing the Path is solid;
6) He does not resort to and rely on the feigning of close affections;
7) He constantly serves as a close friend to beings even up to the point of entering nirvāṇa;
8) Whether personally close or at a distance, his mind remains the same;
9) He does not retreat from good endeavors he has assented to;
10) He does not cut off his kindness for all beings;
11) He does not cut off his compassion for all beings;
12) In his constant pursuit of right Dharma, his mind remains unwearied and does not shrink away from it;
13) He is diligent and never sated in his generation of the mind of vigor;
14) He is possessed of extensive learning and is comprehending of concepts;
15) He is constantly aware of his own faults;
16) He does not deride others for their shortcomings;
17) In all matters he observes or hears, he remains constant in his cultivation of the bodhi mind;

18) In giving, he seeks no reward;
19) His observance of the moral-virtue precepts is not done with a motivation to achieve rebirth in any particular place at all (i.e. he does not do so for the sake of celestial rebirth);
20) He exercises patience toward all beings, remaining free of hatefulness or obstructiveness;
21) He is able to diligently and vigorously cultivate the practice of all roots of goodness;
22) He does not allow himself to take a [celestial] rebirth corresponding to the formless samādhis;
23) His wisdom is inclusive of skillful means;
24) His skillful means are inclusive of the four means of attraction (giving; pleasing words; beneficial actions; joint endeavors);
25) He does not have two different capacities for kindness and sympathy for those who observe moral precepts and those who break moral precepts;
26) He is single-minded in his listening to Dharma;
27) He is single-minded when dwelling in an *araṇya* (a secluded meditation retreat);
28) He does not find pleasure in any of the many different and varying sorts of worldly circumstances;
29) He does not covet or retain any attachment for the Small Vehicle;
30) He perceives that the benefit brought about by the Great Vehicle is in fact great;
31) He departs far from bad [spiritual] friends (i.e. bad gurus);
32) He draws close to good [spiritual] friends (i.e. good gurus).

---

076 – Prior to Definite Stage, As One Fulfills Vows, Skillful Means Restrain Nirvāṇa

Where one has not yet reached "the definite position,"
One holds himself back through the power of skillful means.
Because one has not yet fulfilled his original vows,
In this case too, he refrains from realization of nirvāṇa.

AV Prior to entering the right and definite position, the initial-resolve bodhisattva continues to hold himself back through skillful means as he cultivates the three gates to liberation and proceeds with fulfillment of his original vows. Hence he too refrains from realization of nirvāṇa.

077 – One Rejects Yet Faces Cyclic Existence, Has Faith in but Abstains From Nirvāṇa

Though one abides in the ultimate renunciation for cyclic existence,
He nonetheless confronts cyclic existence directly.
Though one maintains faith and happiness in nirvāṇa,
He nonetheless turns his back on realization of nirvāṇa.

AV Through the three types of blazing vigor, one develops renunciation for cyclic existence, yet restrains the tendency to avoid cyclic existence by contemplating beings as one's own children.

One develops faith and happiness in nirvāṇa, seeing it as a home offering shelter, yet turns away from entering nirvāṇa in order to perfect the wisdom of all-knowledge.

Renunciation for cyclic existence enables faith and happiness in relation to nirvāṇa. Failure to confront cyclic existence directly and failure to turn away from nirvāṇa make one bound to enter nirvāṇa when cultivating the gates to liberation.

TN "Three types of blazing vigor" is probably intended as reference to vigor exercised in physical, verbal, and mental karma.

078 – Dread But Don't End Afflictions; Block Them to Gather Good Karma

One should dread the afflictions,
But should not end the afflictions.
To gather the manifold forms of goodness, one should
Use blocking methods to fend off afflictions.

AV Because they cause cyclic existence, one should dread the negative effect of afflictions while still not ending them entirely, for if one cuts them off, one can't accumulate the provisions for bodhi. Hence the use of blocking methods. By continuing on in cyclic existence, accumulating the roots of goodness, one is able to fulfill one's original vows and eventually reach buddhahood.

TN Although one doesn't entirely end the afflictions, one must still remain vigilant in consistent use of affliction-neutralizing techniques. Failure on this point leads to a massive accumulation of bad karma instead of the accumulation of roots of goodness essential to bodhi.

---

079 – A Bodhisattva Is Better Served by Afflictions than by Nirvāṇa

For the bodhisattva, afflictions accord with his nature.
He is not one who takes nirvāṇa as his very nature.
It is not the case that the burning up of the afflictions
Allows one to generate the seed of bodhi.

AV Nirvāṇa functions as the very nature of the Śrāvaka-Vehicle ārya, for it is by pursuing it that they gain the fruits of that path.

The Buddhas don't take nirvāṇa as their nature, but rather use afflictions in the path to buddhahood, this because the mind resolved on bodhi only arises in the presence of the afflictions.

Two-Vehicles practitioners burn the seed of the bodhi mind and instead establish their resolve independent of the ability to course further in cyclic existence. Because afflictions serve realization of buddhahood, they are integral to it. It is to gain a buddha's body that bodhisattvas refrain from completely abandoning afflictions.

Question: If ending afflictions absolutely prevents buddhahood, why were arhats given predictions in the *Lotus Sutra*?

Response: (See next *śloka*.)

---

080 – Predictions Such as in the Lotus Sutra Were Situation-Specific Expedients

As for the predictions bestowed on those other beings,
These predictions involved specific causal circumstances.
They were solely a function of the Buddha's artfulness
In taking the perfection of skillful means "to the far shore."

AV The causal bases for those (*Lotus Sutra*) predictions, including which beings were being assisted, are known only by the Buddha because:

1) They represent the most extreme expression of the Buddha's training methods.

2) They involve circumstances not shared by any other beings.

3) They involve beings who have eliminated the essential bases for generating the resolve to become a buddha, this by virtue of having already achieved irreversibility in the arhat path.

This circumstance is described in the Sutras as summed up in the following *śloka*.

TN This *śloka* is referring to the predictions of eventual buddhahood bestowed on arhats in the *Lotus Sutra*. The reason for mentioning these in this treatise is because, with the exception of such special cases, it is generally held that, once a practitioner on the individual-liberation arhat-vehicle path reaches that vehicle's "right and definite position," (*samyaktva niyāma*), he thereby passes beyond any further ability to turn away from arhatship and proceed toward buddhahood on the Bodhisattva Path. Absent this explanation, one might think that no difficulties are posed for the realization of buddhahood by coursing in the mind-states of the Śrāvaka-vehicle and Pratyekabuddha-vehicle paths.

The reader may find it useful at this point to refer back to Bhikshu Vaśitva's commentary on *śloka* number thirty-two where the issue of predictions is considered in some detail. It includes comments on just this very sort of prediction, which is one of five types. Of the five types, this one is referred to as a "secretly-intentioned and specially-spoken prediction."

---

081 – Analogies for Incompatibility of Two-Vehicles Irreversibility and Buddhahood

Similes for their plight reference "empty space," "lotus flowers,"
"Precipitous cliffs," and "a deep abyss."
Their realms bar it. Analogies cite "non-virility" and "*kācamaṇi*,"
With an additional comparison made to "burnt seeds."

AV Just as one cannot grow seeds in the midst of empty space, so too one can't achieve buddhahood in the unconditioned. Just as one cannot grow lotus blossoms in the high plains, so too the Śrāvaka-disciples and the Pratyekabuddhas who have entered the unconditioned's "right and definite position" cannot produce the dharmas of buddhahood.

As for "precipitous cliffs," there are two along the path to the city of the wisdom of all-knowledge, the one overhanging the ground of the Śrāvaka-disciples and the other overhanging the ground of the Pratyekabuddhas. If *śrāvaka*-disciples and pratyekabuddhas possessed all-knowledge, [their grounds] would not be like precipitous cliffs for the bodhisattva.

Now, as for the "deep abyss," a well-trained mountain climber can enter a deep abyss and abide there safely whereas someone bereft of such training would die in that deep abyss.

So too, because the bodhisattva is well-cultivated in the practice of the unconditioned, he does not plummet on down into the unconditioned. However, the Śrāvaka-disciples and others have not developed comparable skillfulness as they practice immersion in the unconditioned and hence they plummet on down into the unconditioned.

As for the statement: "Their realms [bar it]," the Śrāvaka-disciples are so tied up in the conditioned that they have no ability to course in the conditioned. Hence they can't generate the mind resolved on bodhi.

As for the comparison to "non-virility," just as an impotent man no longer finds any satisfaction in the sphere of the five desires, so too, those *śrāvaka*-disciples equipped with the dharma of the unconditioned find no further satisfaction in the advantages associated with buddhahood.

As for the comparison to *"kācamaṇi"* (common quartz crystals), just as nobody in the heavens or the world can transform quartz into *vaiḍūrya* gems, so too, even though *śrāvaka*-disciples are equipped with moral-precept training, ascetic practices, samādhis and such, they will still never be able to gain the enlightenment of a buddha.

As for the "burnt seed" simile, just as a burnt seed can never sprout even though planted in soil, watered, and warmed by the sun, so too the Śrāvaka-disciples, having burned up the seeds of the afflictions, can never be born again anywhere in any realm of existence.

Based on such citations from the sutras, one should realize that, once a *śrāvaka*-disciple gains the dharmas of the unconditioned, he will no longer have any ability to aspire to buddhahood.

Question: How should the bodhisattva equipped with the powers cultivate in the midst of beings?

Response: (See next *śloka*.)

TN Nāgārjuna's treatise assumes one is already familiar with the sutras in which these comparisons are made. Hence the *śloka* he provides here is an extremely terse mnemonic intended primarily to remind the reader of the standard sutra-based analogies involved. Since such prior knowledge cannot be assumed for modern-day Dharma students (either East or West), I go ahead and write out the meaning of the *śloka* in full as follows:

> The ability of an irreversible *śrāvaka*-disciple or pratyekabuddha to nourish the seed of buddhahood in their unconditioned state would be like trying to plant seeds in empty space or like trying to grow lotuses on the high plains.

For the bodhisattva, to fall into the paths of *śrāvaka*-disciples or pratyekabuddhas would be like falling over a precipitous cliff to one's death. For the irreversible *śrāvaka*-disciple or pratyekabuddha to aspire to coursing in the Bodhisattva Path would be like someone not trained in mountain climbing to think they could enter and leave deep mountain crevasses or abysses at will rather than be bound to die therein as would certainly be the case.

The realms coursed in by irreversible *śrāvaka*-disciples or pratyeka-buddhas, by their very nature, bar any possibility of begetting the dharmas of buddhahood just as an impotent man would be altogether incapable of gaining satisfaction or begetting a child in the sphere of the five desires and just as nobody can possibly transform common quartz into *vaiḍūrya* gems,

Another analogy compares such a prospect to that of being able to cause a burnt seed to germinate and produce growth.

Nāgārjuna's intent here is not to disparage Two-Vehicles practitioners or the paths they have chosen. Rather it is an attempt to warn those contemplating or already confirmed in the Bodhisattva Path that cultivation of the Two-Vehicles path will lead to a point of no return making it impossible to proceed with the Bodhisattva Path, hence the importance of using skillful means when cultivating techniques such as the three gates to liberation lest one fall away from the Bodhisattva Path.

082 – To Benefit the World, Bring Forth and Treatises, Skills, Sciences, Trades

All of the treatises as well as the specialized skills,
The occult and mundane sciences, and the various trades—
Because they bring benefit to the world,
One brings them forth and establishes them.

AV "Treatises" refers to those on printing, mathematics, metallurgy, medicine, exorcism for ghost-possession, and rescue of poisoning victims. It also refers to treatises on public works, agriculture, horticulture, medicinal herbs, forests, and so forth. And it also includes those devoted to gemology, astronomy, interpretation of dreams, and physiognomy.

Everything beneficial to the world is lost during the deterioration of each kalpa. As the kalpa develops again, these things must be brought forth and established again among people. "Specialized skills" include working with wood, iron, clay, copper, and such. They include all occult and mundane sciences including exorcisms, dealing with insanity, poisoning, digestive afflictions, and so forth. They also include carving, painting, embroidery, weaving, and such, including all of the different sorts of trades. One brings forth and establishes whatever brings benefit and happiness to the world.

---

083 – Adapting to Various Beings, Per One's Vows, One Takes Birth Among Them

Adapting to beings amenable to instruction,
To their worlds, rebirth destinies, and birth circumstances,
As befits one's reflections, one goes directly to them,
And, through power of vows, takes birth among them.

AV Wherever there are beings amenable to instruction, *mahāsattvas* take rebirth among them, adapting to the worlds they inhabit, their particular rebirth destinies, circumstances, physical appearance, and karmic retribution. Relying on the immeasurable minds they generate a resolve propelling them into precisely those situations, this out of a wish to instruct beings in the Path.

---

084 – In the Midst of Evil, Don the Armor and Don't Yield to Either Loathing or Fear

In the midst of all sorts of circumstances rife with evil,
And when among beings prone to guileful flattery and deceit,
One should don one's sturdy armor.
One must not yield to either loathing or fear.

AV When subjected to physical or verbal abuse, guileful flattery, or deceit, one might verge on the conviction that teaching beings is hopeless. One should not be slow to don one's armor. Additionally, one must not be overcome by loathing for cyclic existence or by fearfulness at the length of the Path.

One reflects, "It is not for beings free of these faults that I must strap on this armor, but rather it is precisely for dealing with just such beings."

Question: The cultivation of the bodhisattvas with powers is complete. How should the bodhisattva with no powers proceed?
Response: (As below...)

TN "Armor" may be understood to refer to all of those bodhisattva practices protecting one from generating mental afflictions or bad karmic deeds, in particular: patience (*kṣānti*), so as not to become hateful; moral virtue (*śīla*), so as not to fall into the error of reacting negatively; meditative discipline (*dhyāna*), so as to remain entirely unmoved; equanimity (*upekṣā*), so as to have no special affection for the virtuous or enmity for the evil; wisdom (*prajñā*), so as to realize others' evil toward one is just recompense for one's countless bad karmic deeds in the past, so as to realize that there are ultimately no inherently-existent beings or evil deeds to which one might react, and so as to realize that there is no inherently-existent self which might be the victim of others' evil actions; compassion (*karuṇa*), so as to implement the antidote to hatefulness recommended by the Buddha; and vigor (*vīrya*), so as to not grow weary of the length and difficulty of the Bodhisattva Path.

---

085 – Maintain Pure Intentions, Eschew Guile, Confess Wrongs, Conceal Good Deeds

One equips oneself with supremely pure intentions,
Does not resort to guileful flattery or deception,
Reveals the wrongs of his karmic offenses,
And conceals his many good deeds.

AV "Supremely pure intentions," is a reference to a superior class of motivation and goodness.

(After simply clarifying through restatement the meanings of the straightforward concepts in this *śloka*, Bhikshu Vaśitva continues with a quote he attributes to the Buddha.) The Bhagavān stated, "Guileful flattery is incompatible with bodhi and deception is incompatible with bodhi."

---

086 – Purify Three Karmas, Observe Moral Codes, Allow No Omissions or Slackening

One purifies the karma of body and mouth
And also purifies the karma of the mind.
Cultivating observance of all passages in the moral-code training.
One must not allow any omissions or diminishment in this.

AV To accord with correct cultivation, these bodhisattvas first ensure that the karma of the body, mouth, and mind are made pure and consistent with the path of the ten good karmic deeds regulating killing, stealing, sexual misconduct, ruinous speech, harsh speech, frivolous and lewd speech, divisive speech, covetousness, hatefulness, and erroneous views.

One should also accord with all of the statements contained within moral codes key to liberation, avoiding any instances of deliberate infractions. Where there are deficits in cultivation of the precepts, one becomes unable to still the mind and develop concentration in one's meditation.

TN Particular attention must be paid to Bhikshu Vaśitva's concluding note about deviations from the precepts making it entire impossible to still the mind in meditation. Under such a circumstance, the thoughts will not settle down enough to allow achievement of the one-pointed concentration upon which success in meditation is entirely dependent.

---

087 – Focus on the Object, Still Thoughts in Solitude, Eliminate Obstructive Thoughts

One establishes himself in right mindfulness,
Focuses on the object condition, and stills his thought in solitude.
Having put mindfulness to use as a guard,
The mind becomes free of any obstructive thoughts.

AV Having achieved purity through observance of the moral precepts, one cuts off the five hindrances, and carries on one's cultivation in a pure, isolated location far from the multitude with but little noise, disturbance, mosquitoes, snakes, tigers, thieves, and so forth. It should not be too cold or hot. One does not set up a sleeping cot, but may stand, engage in meditative walking, or may sit in the lotus posture.

One may keep returning one's focus of mindful attention to the tip of the nose or to the forehead, establishing it there. After one has skillfully focused on the single chosen object, if agitated movement arises in the mind, one uses mindfulness to guard the door of the mind, and using this technique to protect the mind, one abandons insurgent thoughts otherwise bound to obstruct the mind.

TN The "five hindrances" (*nīvaraṇa* or *āvaraṇa*) to which Bhikshu Vaśitva refers are: "desire" (*kāma-chanda*); "ill will" (*vyāpāda*); "lethargy and sleepiness" (*styāna-middha*); "excitedness and regretfulness" (*auddhatya-kaukṛtya*); and "[afflicted] doubt" (*vicikitsā*).

On the question of why "lethargy-and-sleepiness" is a dual-component hindrance, Vasubandhu indicates (in Chapter Five of his *Abhidharmakośa Bhāṣyam*) that it is because both "lethargy" and "sleepiness" are nourished by the same five factors (bad omens seen in dreams [*tandrī*]; unhappiness [*arati*]; physical exhaustion [*vijṛmbhikā*]; uneven consumption of food [*bhakte'samatā*]; mental depression [*cetaso līnatva*]), are starved by the same single factor (illuminated perception [*āloka-samjñā*]), and are productive of the same result of mental languor. (See Pruden, *Abhidharmakośa Bhāṣyam* [851–2]).

On the question of why "excitedness-and-regretfulness" is a dual-component hindrance, Vasubandhu indicates that it is because both "excitedness" and "regretfulness" are nourished by the same four factors (ideation regarding relatives, land, immortals, previous pleasures and the associated companions), are starved by the same single factor (calmness), and are productive of the same result of mental agitation. (See Pruden, *Abhidharmakośa Bhāṣyam* [852]).

---

088 – When Discriminating Thoughts Arise, Abandon the Bad, Cultivate the Good

When discriminating thoughts arise,
One should realize which are good and which are unwholesome,
Should forsake any which are not good,
And extensively cultivate those which are good.

AV Bring awareness to bear on any discriminating thought which might arise, abandoning the bad rather than allowing them to increase. Cultivate only those which are good, not allowing any scattered thought. This process is analogous to taking care not to obstruct a lantern's air source when lighting it and setting it out to illuminate a room.

---

089 – When Scattered, Reestablish Focus, Return to the Object, Enforce Stillness

If the mind trained on the object becomes scattered,
One should focus one's mindful awareness,
Return it to that object,
And, whenever movement occurs, immediately cause it to halt.

AV When cultivating meditative concentration, one keeps the mind focused, not allowing scattering. If the mind departs from the object, one should immediately invoke awareness to prevent straying, and return the mind to its focus directly on the object.

This is analogous to using a rope to tie a monkey to a post. One uses the rope of mindfulness to tie the monkey of the mind securely to the post of the object of meditation, doing so in a way that it can only continuously wind itself ever more closely to that post of the meditation object.

---

090 – Refrain from Laxity and Wrong Attachment as They Prevent Concentration

One should refrain from laxity and from wrong attachment
Cultivated with intensity,
For they make it impossible to maintain concentration.
One should therefore remain constant in one's cultivation.

AV "Laxity" refers to desisting from stringency in one's efforts. "Wrong attachment" refers to a type of grasping which is unwholesome. Development of meditative absorption entails restraint from both of these. Such departures from correct practice make it impossible to abide in meditative absorption.

TN Many unwholesome meditation mind states may arise when cultivating meditative discipline, some arising from karmic propensities rooted in the past, some having to do with unskillfulness in the present, and some having to do with exogenous factors. (See my translation of the Sui Dynasty Dhyāna Master Zhiyi's *Essentials of Buddhist Meditation* for a reasonably comprehensive discussion of these issues.)

If one allows oneself to become involved in these mind states, one may experience proliferation and intensification of afflictions. Examples of this vulnerability include attachment to powerful psychic phenomena and attachment to intensely blissful sensual pleasures arising in meditation as the subtle energies manifest in meditation. Averting any attention to these phenomena (even more so "cultivating them with intensity") tends to magnify the afflicted-attachment and distraction-invoking aspects and tends to make them more chronically present. This inevitably kills concentration, thereby straightaway defeating the right-Dharma rationale behind one's taking up the cultivation of meditation in the first place.

It is for this reason that the 25,000-line *Great Perfection of Wisdom Sutra* and Nāgārjuna himself state, "It is on account of remaining unattached to the delectable flavor of meditative states that one becomes able to achieve the perfection of dhyāna meditation." (See my translation *Nāgārjuna on the Six Perfections*, at the very beginning of the chapters devoted to the perfection of dhyāna meditation.)

091 – Even Two-Vehicles' Men Focused on Self-Benefit Insist on Vigor in Meditation

Even were one to take up the vehicle of the Śrāvakas
Or the vehicle of the Pratyekabuddhas,
And hence practice solely for one's own benefit,
One would still not relinquish the enduring practice of vigor.

AV Even those dedicated solely to their own self-benefit and nirvāṇa find it necessary to strive both day and night, never relinquishing enduring and solid vigor as the goad to pursue diligent cultivation of meditation.

TN Nāgārjuna warns in the most emphatic terms that any sort of meaningful progress in meditation is entirely dependent upon nearly heroic levels of vigor, this in the "Perfection of Vigor" section of his *Exegesis on the Great Perfection of Wisdom Sutra* (*Mahāprajñāpāramitā Upadeśa*). He also makes a point of clarifying therein that this is precisely why "vigor" is listed immediately before "meditation" in the standard Mahāyāna ordering of the six perfections. (See my complete translation: *Nāgārjuna on the Six Perfections*.)

092 – How Much the Less Might a Bodhisattva Fail to Generate Infinite Vigor

How much the less could it be that a great man
Committed to liberate both himself and all others
Might somehow fail to generate
A measure of vigor a thousand *koṭīs* times greater?

AV Given that the bodhisattva has committed himself to liberating all beings, how could he not generate vigor infinitely more robust than Two-Vehicles practitioners? That he would inevitably do so flows from vowing to devote as much effort to liberating others from cyclic existence as he devotes to liberating himself.

093 – Don't Pursue Other Practice Half-Time or Conjoint Practice of Other Paths

As for cultivating some other practice half the time
Or simultaneously practicing some other path,
One should not do this when cultivating meditative concentration.
One should rather focus exclusively on a single objective condition.

AV One should rather devote oneself solely to skillfully focusing on a single object as one practices a single type of meditative concentration. The mind then focuses on whichever single objective phenomenon one has chosen. Thus one must refrain from directing it toward any other circumstance.

---

094 – Covet Neither Body nor Life as the Body is Bound for Destruction

One must not indulge any covetousness regarding the body
And must not cherish even one's own life.
Even were one to allow any protectiveness toward this body,
It is but a dharma bound in the end to rot away.

AV One should reflect on the body as a mere collection of skin, flesh, blood, sinews, bones, marrow, and so forth, all of which, even were it to last a hundred years, is finally bound to rot. One should reflect on one's life as bound to come to an end.

Still, one must not indulge any laxness, but rather should strive vigorously to achieve through cultivation of the Path whatever might be possible while endowed with health and strength.

---

095 – Never Coveting Offerings, Reverence, or Fame, Strive Urgently to Fulfill Vows

One must never develop a covetous attachment
To offerings, reverence from others, or fame.
Rather one should strive diligently to fulfill one's vows,
Acting with the urgency of one whose turban has caught fire.

AV One proceeds in this as when traveling through the wilds, intent on progressing, not obsessing on physical incidentals or life concerns. Were someone to make an offering, express reverence, or bandy one's name about, one wouldn't dally over any of that. Now, intent on fulfilling vows, one pursues swift and diligent practice with the urgency of one whose turban has caught fire.

---

096 – Resolutely Seize Victory, Not Waiting till Later as Survival Isn't Guaranteed

Acting resolutely and immediately, pull forth the supreme benefit.
In this, one cannot wait for tomorrow.
Tomorrow is too distant a time,
For how can one ensure survival even for the blink of an eye?

AV When practicing as intensely as if one's turban had caught fire, tomorrow is seen as too distant. Where some action will provide the most supreme benefit [to progress on the Path], one proceeds with resolve and immediacy, reflecting, "How can one guarantee survival even for the blink of an eye. I must not put this off till tomorrow."

---

097 – Established in Right Livelihood, Be Mindful and Free of Preferences in Eating

Having established oneself in right livelihood,
When eating, it is as if consuming the flesh of a cherished son.
One must not indulge in either affection for or disapproval of
Whatever food one has taken for the meal.

AV The bhikshu devoted to meditation obtains his alms meal in accordance with Dharma and entertains toward it neither any relishing nor any disdain, but rather maintains mindfulness of it as solely a means to preserve his life. The text alludes to the story of the couple traveling in the wilderness forced to eat the flesh of a son who had just died, this to illustrate the correct attitude toward taking meals when preserving one's focus on the meditation.

---

098 – Review One's Monastic Deeds and Accordance with the Ten Dharmas Sutra

For what purpose has one left the home life?
Have I finished what is to be done or not?
Reflect now on whether or not one is doing the work,
Doing so as described in the *Ten Dharmas Sutra*.

AV One should carry out analytic contemplation on these topics:

1) "For what purpose did I take up the practice of the monastic? Was it to achieve the goals of a monk or not?"

2) "If to achieve the goals of a monk, have I accomplished them, not yet accomplished them, or am I just now accomplishing them?"

3) "If one has not yet begun to accomplish them or is just now accomplishing them, then vigor should be brought to the work."

4) "Having left the householder's life, then I should qualify as no longer being of that sort. I should in fact be duly carrying forth this different life."

5) "Have I succeeded or not in adhering to the moral precepts in a manner beyond reproach? Would someone well-versed in these matters approve or disapprove my performance on this account?"

6) "I have already taken up a different appearance from those toward whom I have had affectionate relationships and hence no longer share the same basis for carrying on my life. Still, I am bound

to undergo the fruits of my karmic actions and exist in an intimate relationship with my karma."

7) "How do I pass my days and nights? Do I or do I not delight in cultivating realization of emptiness and quiescence?"

8) "Have I or have I not come into the possession of the dharmas of a superior man?"

9) "Have I or have I not been able to succeed in gaining the superior knowledge and vision of the Āryas?"

10) "When interviewed in the future by another man who has adopted these pure practices, will I or will I not have reason to be ashamed?"

This monk who herein devotes himself to cultivation of meditative concentration should reflect repeatedly on the ten dharmas.

099 – Contemplate Impermanence and Non-self, Abandoning Demonic Karma

Contemplate conditioned phenomena as impermanent,
As devoid of self, and as devoid of anything belonging to a self.
One must become aware of and withdraw from
All forms of demonic karmic activity.

AV "Conditioned phenomena" are those existing through the coming together of causes and conditions. Having such bases, they are therefore impermanent and devoid of anything belonging to a self. Being impermanent, they are marked by suffering. Being marked by suffering and the inability to exert any independence in their own development, they are therefore devoid of self.

"Demonic karma" is that through which one experiences displeasure, mental scatteredness or confusion, laxness, or obstacles in relation to the quest for bodhi and sutras teaching the six perfections. Whether the circumstances are self-generated or generated by some other source, it is essential to become aware of any such demonic karmic activity and withdraw from it. Then, having abandoned it, one must ensure that there is no basis for its being able to continue on independently of one's own active involvement in it.

———

TN Dhyāna Master Zhiyi devotes an entire chapter to the issue of demons, demonic karma, how they manifest, and how their influences may be countered in his *Essentials for Practicing Calming-and-Insight and Dhyāna Meditation*. I have translated that entire work and am publishing it as *The Essentials of Buddhist Meditation*.

100 – Generate Vigor in the Thirty-Seven Wings of Enlightenment

Generate energetic diligence in order to cultivate
The roots, powers, limbs of enlightenment,
Bases of spiritual powers, right severances, the Path,
And the four stations of mindfulness.

AV The "five roots" are: faith, vigor, mindfulness, concentration, and wisdom.

The "five powers" are those very same five roots once fully developed.

The "seven limbs of enlightenment" consist of: mindfulness, dharma-selectivity, vigor, joy, light easefulness, concentration, and equanimity.

The "four bases of spiritual power" are: zeal, vigor, single-mindedness, and contemplative thought, this when they are brought to bear in meditative concentration.

The "four bases of right severance" involve: not allowing not-yet-arisen evil and unwholesome dharmas to come into existence, cutting off already-arisen evil and unwholesome dharmas, causing not-yet-arisen good dharmas to arise, causing already-arisen good dharmas to continue abiding, developing zeal, generating diligence, focusing the mind, and bringing forth vows.

The "four bases of right severance" are: developing zeal, generating diligence, focusing the mind, and bringing forth vows.

The "eight-fold path of the Āryas" consists of: right views, right mental discriminations, right speech, right karmic action, right livelihood, right effort in one's actions, right mindfulness, and right meditative concentration.

The "four stations of mindfulness" are: the body, the [six categories of] feelings [associated with the six sense faculties], the thoughts, and dharmas as phenomena.

One should generate intensely energetic diligence in the cultivation and practice of these thirty-seven factors assisting the realization of bodhi.

———————

TN In his listing of the thirty-seven wings of enlightenment, one may notice that Bhikshu Vaśitva lists not thirty-seven, but rather a total of forty-one components. However, this is merely because "the four bases of right severance" has developed in Buddhist doctrine as an alternative list to "the four right efforts." Bhikshu Vaśitva simply lists all eight of these list components, but places them all here under the "four bases of right severance."

It is interesting to note that such a confirmed Mahāyānist as Nāgārjuna points to the thirty-seven wings of bodhi as fundamental and essential components of Buddhist practice. Although this should be obvious, some latter-day advocates of the Great-Vehicle path have tended at times to diminish their importance, championing the various iterations of the perfections in their stead, almost as if the perfections and the thirty-seven wings were mutually exclusive practice modes.

Nāgārjuna comments on this issue in his commentary on the 25,000-line *Sutra on the Great Perfection of Wisdom*, pointing out that, absent competence in the thirty-seven wings of bodhi, there is no way that a bodhisattva would be able to endure on the Mahāyāna path for countless lifetimes without falling away, back into the karma-bound sufferings of cyclic existence.

See my translation of this extensive discussion entitled *Nāgārjuna on the Thirty-Seven Wings of Enlightenment*. Here is a brief selection from that text:

> Furthermore, where is it said that the thirty-seven wings are only dharmas of the Śrāvaka-disciples and the Pratyekabuddhas and are not the path of the Bodhisattvas? Within this very *Prajñāpāramitā* [*Sutra*], in the chapter entitled "The Mahāyāna," the Buddha discussed the four stations of mindfulness and so forth until we come to the eight-fold path of the Āryas. Nor is it stated anywhere within the three repositories of the Mahāyāna canon that the thirty-seven wings are solely dharmas of the Small Vehicle.
>
> It was on account of his great compassion that the Buddha proclaimed the thirty-seven-winged path to nirvāṇa. It is in correspondence to the vows of beings and the causes and conditions of beings that each of them then takes up his [own particular] path. Those persons who seek that of the Śrāvaka-disciples gain the path of the Śrāvaka-disciples. Those persons who plant the good roots of the Pratyekabuddha gain the path of the Pratyekabuddha. Those who seek the path of the Buddha gain the path of the Buddha. This corresponds to one's original vows, to the acuity or dullness of one's faculties, and to the possession or non-possession of the great compassion.

---

101 – Focus Analytic Contemplation on the Mind as Source of Good and Root of Evil

The mind may serve as a source for the repeated generation
Of good deeds bestowing benefit and happiness
Or it may instead serve as the root of all sorts of evil and turbidity.
One should make it the focus of skillful analytic contemplation.

AV If subdued, guarded, and restrained, the mind creates benefit
and happiness for others. If not, it becomes the root of evil and turbid actions benefiting no one.

On realizing this, one should subject the mind to analytic
contemplation through which one observes its marks of production and destruction, its unfindability inwardly, outwardly, or in
between, its unfindability in the past, future, or present, its coming
from nowhere and going nowhere, its failure to abide even for the
briefest moment, and its similarity to a magically-conjured illusion.
One carries on these analytic contemplations to enhance the quality
of one's practice.

---

102 – Contemplate With Great Concern Daily Increase and Decrease of Good Dharmas

"From one day to the next, what increase has occurred
In my cultivation of good dharmas?"
"Also, what diminishment has occurred in this?"
Those should be the contemplations of utmost concern.

AV The Buddha himself instructed us to carry out this contemplation, specifically regarding those good dharmas able to give birth
to bodhi including giving and the rest [of the perfections]. One
should always focus detailed contemplation on these matters each
and every day, bringing this matter up time and time again.

TN Bhikshu Vaśitva quotes the Buddha as stipulating the contemplation topic as focusing on "giving and the rest." Because "giving"
is the first in the standard order of the six perfections, we should
infer the other five as being integral to the contemplation. Hence,
we should contemplate: "To what extent have giving, moral virtue,
patience, vigor, meditative concentration, and wisdom increased?
To what extent has my practice of the six perfections deteriorated?"

103 – Never Indulge Thoughts of Stinginess or Jealousy over Others' Good Fortune

Whenever one observes someone else experiencing an increase
In offerings, reverences, or reputation,
Even the most subtle thoughts of stinginess and jealously
Should never be indulged.

AV One should avoid any tendency to feel a sense of stinginess or jealousy while contemplating thus: "I too could tend to delight in receiving offerings, robes, food-and-drink, bedding, medicines, and such. I too could tend to delight in expressions of reverence by laity and monastics. And I too could tend to delight in having perfected dharmas which others find praiseworthy."

TN Bhikshu Vaśitva is suggesting here that, rather than being averse to someone else's gaining such things, one should instead cultivate a form of concurring sympathetic joy whereby one delights in another's good fortune and also feels a sympathetic personal identity with their being mentally moved by such things, this in spite of the fact that the ideal practitioner of the Path would remain entirely immune to feeling any particular pleasure or displeasure regarding the presence or absence of such incidentals.

104 – Ignore Sense Realms as if Dull, Blind, Deaf, and Mute, Yet Roar the Lion's Roar

One should not cherish any aspect of the objective realms,
But rather should act as if dull-witted, blind, mute, and deaf.
Still, when timely, respond by roaring the lion's roar,
Frightening off the non-Buddhist deer.

AV When observing others receiving an increase in offerings, reverence, and reputation, one should not cherish any aspect of the sense realms, but rather carries on a type of practice wherein one acts as if dull-witted, blind, mute, and deaf.

Where one possesses the ability, one should still use right Dharma to dispel others' delusions. When the time is right for rectifying someone's attachments to wrong view, one should "frighten off the deer of the non-Buddhist traditions" by roaring "the lion's roar," thus preserving the dominance of correct teachings.

TN Bhikshu Vaśitva notes that the treatise transitions here from explaining cultivation of the mind to explaining cultivation of the marks [of a buddha's body]. That discussion takes place across the course of the next eight *ślokas*.

___

105 – Welcome, Escort, and Revere the Venerable, Assisting All Dharma Endeavors

In welcoming them on arrival and escorting them off as they go,
One should be reverential toward those worthy of veneration.
In all endeavors associated with the Dharma,
One should follow along, participate, and contribute assistance.

___

AV Through respect displayed by offering flowers or garlands on hearing Dharma explained, by repairing *caityas*, and by doing other Dharma works, one gains [a buddha-body's] mark of the wheel on the hands and feet, a sign foretelling a large retinue.

___

106 – Liberate Beings and Cultivate Special Skills, Training Self and Teaching Others

One rescues and liberates beings bound to be killed.
One's goodness increases and never decreases.
One well cultivates karmic works involving the sciences and skills,
Training in them oneself while also teaching them to others.

___

AV Through rescuing those bound to be killed, one gains [the buddha body's] marks of long fingers, heels which are level and upright, and an especially erect body, signs foretelling future enjoyment of a long lifespan.

Through ever increasing good dharmas and not allowing them to decrease, one becomes bound to gain the [buddha-body's] marks of having high ankle bones shaped like shells and body hairs directed in the superior direction, signs foretelling the future possession of undiminishing Dharma.

Through cultivating knowledge of the sciences and specialized skills, studying them oneself and teaching them to others, one becomes bound to gain [a buddha-body's] mark of having calves like those of an *aineya*, [the black antelope], a sign foretelling the future ability to swiftly attract others [to the Dharma].

___

107 – Firmly Adopt Good Dharmas and Cultivate the Four Means of Attraction

Adopt all of the supremely good dharmas,
Through persistent and solid practice.
Cultivate the four means of attraction,
Making gifts of robes and food and drink.

AV Through devoted practice of good dharmas, one gains the bud-dha-body's mark of solidly planted feet, a sign foretelling the future ability to carry out one's chosen work.

Through cultivating the four means of attraction (giving, pleasing speech, beneficial actions, and joint endeavors), one gains the buddha-body's mark of webbed junctions at the roots of the fingers and toes, another sign foretelling the future ability to swiftly attract others to Dharma.

Through giving fine food, drink, and clothing, one gains a bud-dha-body's marks of soft hands and feet and the seven prominences, both of which are signs foretelling inevitability of future possession of those endowments in accordance with one's wishes.

TN As noted in the commentary, the four means of attraction (*catvāri-saṃgraha-vastūni*) are: giving (*dāna-saṃgraha*), pleasing discourse (*priya-vādita-saṃgraha*), beneficial actions (*artha-caryā-saṃgraha*), and accompaniment of others in joint endeavors (*samānārthatā-saṃgraha*). These are four essential altruistic stratagems through which the bodhisattva successfully influences beings to more readily accept and cultivate Dharma where they might not otherwise be well dis-posed to do so.

---

108 – Be Generous to Almsmen, Unite Kin and Clan, Give Dwellings and Possessions

Do not turn away from those begging for alms.
Facilitate the uniting of close relatives.
Prevent estrangement between those of the same clan.
Make gifts of dwellings and of material possessions as well.

AV Through generosity to almsmen in a manner befitting one's resources, one gains a buddha-body's mark of straight and round arms and thighs, a sign foretelling future possession of the ability to freely subdue whomever must be subdued.

Bringing together relatives, retinue, and friends, preventing estrangement, and reconciling the already estranged, one gains a buddha-body's mark of genital ensheathing, a sign foretelling the future possession of many [Dharma] sons.

Through giving dwellings, possessions, fine bedding, robes, halls, temple buildings, and such, one gains a buddha-body's marks of a gold-colored appearance and smooth skin, signs foretelling future endowment with fine possessions and dwellings.

109 – Provide for Parents, Relatives, and Friends Appropriately and Deferentially

As for one's father, mother, relatives, and friends,
Provide them circumstances befitting their station.
Wherever one has given them such a suitable situation,
Treat them as supreme and independent sovereigns.

AV Through providing appropriate circumstances for *upādhyāyas*, *ācāryas*, parents, brothers, and others and then treating them with great deference, one gains a buddha-body's marks of a single hair in each hair pore and the white-hair mid-brow mark, signs foretelling future peerlessness.

110 – Servants Are Addressed with Kindness, Adopted, Esteemed, and Cared For

Although there may be yet others who are servants,
One speaks to them with goodness and, in effect, adopts them.
One should accord them the highest esteem
And provide them with medicines and treatment for all illnesses.

AV Through providing retainers with medicines, treatment for all illnesses, rest, assistance with needs, and food and drink, one gains a buddha-body's marks of having the area of the back between the shoulders even and of having the most superior sense of taste, signs foretelling a future with but little illness.

111 – Be Foremost in Good Karma, Sublime and Right in Speech, and Generous to All

Be the first to act, taking the lead in good karmic deeds,
Speaking with smooth and sublime words,
Being skillful in discourse guided by right intention,
And having no one above or below to whom gifts are not given.

AV "Being the first to act, taking the lead in good karmic deeds" refers to the giving of gardens, groves, meeting halls, wells, ponds, food and drink, flowers and garlands, bridges, Sangha dwellings, walking areas, and so forth, encouraging others on the one hand and personally pushing ahead with these works on the other.

Through giving going beyond the contributions of others, one gains a buddha body's marks of a round girth like the *nyagrodha* tree and the prominence on the crown of the head, both of which are signs foretelling future overlordship.

Through "speaking with smooth and sublime words" that are

truthful and agreeable, one gains a buddha body's marks of a broad and long tongue and a voice imbued with the "brahman sound," both of which are signs foretelling future possession of the voice perfect in speech graced by two groups of five special qualities.

Through "being skillful in discourse guided by right intention," one gains a buddha body's mark of having lion-like jaws, a sign foretelling the future inevitability that one will speak with pleasing words.

Through comporting oneself in accordance with the Dharma while also comporting oneself in a way which is uniformly equal in the treatment of others one gains a buddha-body's marks of uniformly even teeth and teeth which are smooth, both of which are signs foretelling future leadership of a following of those who are both good and pure.

---

112 – Avoid Harm or Disapproval; Regard Others with Kindness and as Good Friends

Avoid any harm to the retinue of others.
Instead regard beings with the eye of kindness.
Neither may one course in disapproving thoughts.
Instead treat everyone as a good relative or friend.

AV Maintain a mind that holds beings dear, teaches them with kindness, draws them in, and accepts them. Through regarding them with an eye free of covetousness, hatefulness, or delusion, one gains a buddha-body's marks of possessing blue eyes and having eyelashes like the king of bulls, signs foretelling the future ability to regard all with the eye of kindliness.

Having explained the causes for the thirty-two marks, we now explain the various other sorts of bodhisattva practices.

TN Bhikshu Vaśitva makes no comment on Nāgārjuna's instruction to "avoid any harm to the retinue of others." This may well refer to attempting to draw into one's own following the disciples of some other teacher of Dharma, perhaps based on jealousy, perhaps based on arrogance, or perhaps based on either well-founded or baseless disapproval of some aspect of that Dharma teacher's abilities. In any case, chipping away at the respect others hold for some other ethically pure teacher of Dharma would not represent the highest expression of the Bodhisattva Path. Hence the warning to avoid it.

---

113 – Act Straightaway in Conformity with Pronouncements, Thus Inspiring Faith

One should accord with the words he speaks,
Following them straightaway with concordant actions.
If one acts immediately in accordance with his words,
Others will be inclined then to develop faith.

AV The effect of immediately behaving in accordance with one's words is that others will consequently be inclined to promptly believe and accept whichever teachings are offered.

---

114 – Be Protective of Dharma, Observant of Neglect, and Inclined to Adorn Stupas

One should support and protect the Dharma
And should discover any instances of neglect,
Even going so far as to build canopies graced by gold and jewels
Spreading over and covering the *caityas*.

AV "One should be supportive and protective of this Dharma. Where there may be neglectful beings who have turned their backs on the Dharma, one should adopt skillful means for them as well, means whereby one might be made aware of such cases and then influence them to turn back toward the Dharma."

This support and protection should extends to sites occupied by *caityas* commemorating the Tathāgata where one may use all sorts of precious adornments to grace a net-like canopy spreading out over it. Such actions are causes for completeness and perfection in one's future buddha body's major and minor marks.

TN A *caitya* is a memorial monument, mound, or stupa commemorating a holy place or person. Sometimes they are located where the remains of a realized being were cremated (as with the cremation stupa close to Kusinigar) and sometimes they are located where the relics and ashes are currently preserved and made the focus of commemorative reverence.

When he mentions "neglectful beings who have turned their back on the Dharma," Bhikshu Vaśitva is perhaps referring to monastics occupying temple or stupa facilities, but not seeing to their maintenance in a manner appropriately respectful to and protective of Dharma. Under such a circumstance, a follower of the Bodhisattva Path might look into the matter and see what if anything might be done to offer support in restoration of the facilities and perhaps even, through the fourth of the four means of attraction ("joint endeavors"), he might simultaneously buoy renewed enthusiasm for more attentive cultivation of the Path.

---

115 – Facilitate Marriages, Present the Bride, Praise the Buddha, and Give Mālās

For those wishing to obtain a maiden mate,
See to her adornment and assist in her presentation.
Speak to the parties about the qualities of the Buddha
And then give prayer beads gleaming in varying hues.

AV Through the giving involved in formalizing a marriage, one produces the future effect of gaining whatever one dearly seeks.

Through praising the qualities of the Buddha with lovely and sublime phrasings pleasing to the minds of the couple and their guests, one gains in future lives a voice pure in all its aspects.

Through presenting gleaming prayer beads made from fine stones pleasing the mind's eye, one contributes to the future effect of having a buddha body replete with all of the fine subsidiary physical characteristics.

---

116 – Create Buddha Images and Cultivate the Six Dharmas of Community Harmony

Create images of the Buddha
Sitting upright atop supremely fine lotus blossoms
And cultivate common delight and happiness
Through adherence to the six dharmas of community harmony.

AV Through making fine buddha images, one gains the future ability to generate transformation bodies and the future ability to gain the body of a buddha.

Through adherence to the six dharmas of harmony and respectfulness of monastics united through common observance of *brahmacarya* (strict celibacy), one enables future acquisition of a retinue invulnerable to ruin by non-Buddhist traditions.

TN "The six dharmas of harmony and respectfulness" pertain to six identities in the monastic community united through common observance of *brahmacarya*:

1) Kindness in physical karma.
2) Kindness in verbal karma.
3) Kindness in mental karma.

4) Common and equal sharing of offerings contributed to the monastic community by the laity.

5) Common and identical monastic moral-code adherence as defined by the Buddha.

6) Common and identical adherence to right view as defined by the Buddha.

Although the Buddha clearly formulated this set of bases for harmony and mutual respect with the monastic community in mind, there is no reason that an analogue version of the same six dharmas could not serve as a useful community-unity reference for lay Buddhists, this by simply stipulating the five lay precepts or the ten good karmic deeds as the operative standard for what is agreed to constitute basic moral excellence.

(The five precepts proscribe killing, stealing, sexual misconduct, lying, and intoxicants, whereas the ten good karmic deeds involve abstention from killing, stealing, sexual misconduct, lying, harsh speech, divisive speech, frivolous or lewd speech, covetousness, hatefulness, and wrong views.)

---

117 – Make Offerings to All and Never Slander the Buddha or Teachers of Dharma

Of those who may be given offerings, none are not given offerings.
Even for the sake of preserving one's life, one still does not slander
The Dharma spoken by the Buddha
Or the person who expounds the Dharma.

AV There should be representatives able to act as stewards in looking after offerings, namely the *upādhyāyas* or the *ācāryas*, the parents, elder brothers, or others of this sort. As for "none not given offerings," there are none to whom one does not show reverence. One scrupulously avoids slander, slighting, or deception directed toward the Dharma or those who expound it, this so as to preserve one's own requisites for bodhi.

TN The phrase "those who may be given offerings" may seem confusing if we assume that this option is open to anyone. However, in a community of monks observing the strictest traditions, none will personally even touch money or other valuables (such as gold or silver). In such a situation, an offering to the community at large might only properly be accepted on its behalf by the lay attendant of a senior monastic holding a position of responsibility in the community (such as attendants of the *upādhyāyas* or *ācāryas* mentioned by Bhikshu Vaśitva).

In the case of an offering intended to benefit an individual monk not living in community, but rather living in a hermitage or other solitary situation, the offering might have to be made to a trusted lay attendant, or in the absence of same, might have to be made to close relatives such as parents or an elder brother who could be trusted to use it in benefiting the monastic recipient.

As for the extreme scrupulousness regarding avoiding slander of the Dharma or one who expounds Dharma (as recommended by Nāgārjuna), and regarding avoiding merely slighting or deceiving one who speaks Dharma (as warned against by Bhikshu Vaśitva), one should realize that such karma not only threatens the goodness imbuing one's own requisites for bodhi, it also establishes causes for future-life difficulty in ever being able to encounter the monastic community or the Dharma again.

---

118 – Donate to Teaching Masters and Their Stupas, See to Preservation of Scripture

Gold and jewels are distributed among teaching masters
And also among the *caityas* of teaching masters.
If there are those who forget what is to be recited,
One assists their remembrance, enabling them to stay free of error.

AV Such assets are distributed to the teaching masters and to the *caityas* commemorating teaching masters.

The bodhisattva possesses a samādhi known as "manifesting in the direct presence of the Buddhas" which is cultivated for life-after-life hearing and retention of Dharma. These bodhisattvas refresh the memories of those preserving the teachings by recitation. Through this, they gain future endowment with the ability to never forget the mind resolved on bodhi and the ability to have powerful memory.

TN There is no inherent implication in either Nāgārjuna's *śloka* or Bhikshu Vaśitva's commentary that those specializing in teaching Dharma would have any personal interest or need to possess "gold and jewels." On the contrary, they are most likely to be most well aware of the karmic dangers involved in their misuse and most likely to understand their correct use in serving the interests of the Three Jewels, the Buddha, the Dharma, and the Monastic Sangha.

As for the passage devoted to faithful remembrance of scriptures, it may be helpful to remember that important scriptures were traditionally committed to memory by monastics, especially by those who specialized in teaching the Dharma. This was done perhaps primarily because the teachings were most effectively internalized in this way, but also because palm-leaf copies were comparatively rare, fragile, and prone to rapid destruction by white ants.

Bhikshu Vaśitva is likely referring here to the samādhis of the sixth bodhisattva ground, the ground known as "the ground of present manifestation" (*abhimukha-bhūmi*).

---

119 – Let Reflection Precede Action; Have no Faith in Non-Buddhists, Gods, or Spirits

When one has not yet reflected on the right course of action,
One must not be impulsive and must not simply emulate others.
As for the non-Buddhists, gods, dragons, and spirits,
One must not invest one's faith in any of them.

AV Physical, verbal, or mental actions not preceded by reflection and undertaken through impetuousness or imitation occasion later regret. Avoid developing any faith in non-Buddhist traditions, deities, dragons (*nāgas*), *yakṣas*, *gandharvas* and such.

TN Nāgārjuna is not insisting that one should fail to believe in the existence of "gods, dragons (*nāgas*), and spirits." On the contrary, those classes of entities *do* exist and often enough *do* have enough in the way of low-grade powers to seriously interfere with a practitioner's mental clarity, especially in cases where one has voluntarily entered into some sort of psycho-spiritual relationship with them.

What all of these entities have in common is a complete inability to extricate their followers from the endless karma-bound sufferings of cyclic existence. Hence Nāgārjuna's admonition: "One must not invest one's faith in any of them."

As regards Bhikshu Vaśitva's advice to avoid nominally "spiritual" activities not preceded by careful reflection and not clearly based directly on the Buddha's teaching, the Buddha admonished the monastic community to avoid not only those actions which he had specifically forbidden in the moral codes, but also to avoid those actions which were semblances of what was specifically forbidden. Where we find no clear basis in classic Southern Tradition or Mahāyāna teachings for certain practices which may have become popular after the first one thousand years post-nirvāṇa, a certain amount of circumspection is well justified lest one fall into practices which are essentially non-Buddhist and hence not really conducive to liberation at all. An obvious example would be propitiation of ghosts, wrathful deities, and so forth. There are of course many other examples of which the serious Dharma student will already be well aware.

120 – Make the Mind Penetratingly Sharp Like Vajra and as Immovable as a Mountain

One's mind should be like vajra,
Able to penetrate all dharmas.
One's mind should also be like a mountain,
Remaining unmoved in any circumstance.

AV Through the power of wisdom, one's mind penetratingly understands all worldly and world-transcending dharmas in accordance with their nature and reality. Being like a mountain, it cannot be moved by any of the eight worldly dharmas.

TN The eight worldly dharmas are: gain and loss; disgrace and esteem; praise and blame; suffering and happiness.

121 – Delight in Transcendent Words, Abandon Worldly Talk, Inspire Merit in Others

Delight in world-transcending discourse
And do not take pleasure in worldly words.
Personally adopt all manner of meritorious qualities.
One should then influence others to adopt them as well.

AV One should find delight in discourse devoted to the Three Jewels, to the six perfections, or to the grounds of the bodhisattvas, *śrāvakas*, and pratyekabuddhas, this while finding no pleasure in discourse devoted to worldly topics or tending to increase worldliness, discourse such as relates to desire, hatred, and delusion.

One should adopt qualities such as inhere in the moral precepts, the *dhūta* (ascetic) practices, or other praiseworthy dharmas, this while influencing others to adopt them as well.

TN Bhikshu Vaśitva mentions the *dhūta* practices. These are relatively ascetic forms of Dharma practice requiring intense dedication to uphold. Examples include: abiding in a charnel field; living in solitude in a hermitage; living out in the open; living beneath a tree, usually only for a fixed amount of time after one must move to another tree; eating but one meal each day, consuming it before noon; eating that one meal at a single sitting; eating a fixed amount in that one meal; having eaten the single meal before noon, not drinking beverages other than water after noon; wearing only robes made of cast-off rags; only wearing the three robes; only consuming alms-round food; and only sitting, never lying down.

The difference between the Buddhist set of twelve *dhūta* practices and the asceticism of the non-Buddhists is that the *dhūta* practices all actually benefit some aspect or another of one's spiritual practice, bringing about more rapid progress in the development of essential spiritual qualities. This sets them apart from useless forms of asceticism found in non-Buddhist traditions, practices such as: abiding on a bed of nails; wandering around naked, covered with ashes; standing on one leg; never cutting one's hair; and attempting to wash away one's evil karma simply by washing in the Ganges River.

---

122 – Cultivate Five Liberation Bases, Ten Impurity Reflections, Eight Realizations

Cultivate the five bases of liberation.
Cultivate the ten reflections on impurity.
The eight realizations of great men
Should also be the focus of analytic contemplation and cultivation.

AV The "five bases of liberation" are: listening to Dharma explained by others; explaining Dharma for others; reciting the Dharma from memory; analytic contemplation of Dharma; grasping specific aspects of any given meditative absorption.

The "ten reflections on impurity" counteract lust and involve reflection on: the distended corpse; the corpse blue from stagnant blood; the purulent, rotting corpse; the oozing corpse; the gnawed corpse; the dismembered corpse; the scattered corpse; the blood-smeared corpse; the mangled corpse; the skeletal corpse.

The "eight realizations of great men" stipulate that the following are genuine Dharma and their opposites are not: but little desire; being easily satisfied; abiding at a distance from the hustle-and-bustle; vigor; mindfulness of Dharma; entering meditative absorption; wisdom; not finding enjoyment in frivolous discourse. Of these one adopts the salutary and does away with their opposites.

▣ Bhikshu Vaśitva's list of the ten reflections on the impure records an only slightly different list from the commonly-encountered list of nine reflections deriving from the *Mahāprajñāpāramitā Sūtra*. His list does not include the burned corpse of the list of nine, and adds the "oozing" corpse and "dismembered" corpse not in the list of nine. For more on this from Nāgārjuna himself, see my translation of his discussion of this practice entitled *Nāgārjuna on the Nine Reflections*.

Bhikshu Vaśitva's list of the eight realizations of great men is standard, but differs slightly from the Mahāyāna sutra of that name translated in the middle of the Second Century by Tripiṭaka Master An Shigao (T17.0779.715b). Bhikshu Vaśitva's list accords with the version recorded by Nāgārjuna in his treatise on the ten bodhisattva grounds (T26.1521.92c) and with the *Āgamas* (T01.0001.55c).

The scripture translated by An Shigao describing eight realizations of great men is more profound in terms of the breadth and depth of topics mentioned and in its descriptiveness of the Path. Topics it mentions upon which the *Āgama* list is silent are: impermanence, suffering, emptiness, and non-self; the practice of giving; equal regard for friends and adversaries; absence of grudge-bearing thought; non-hatred of evil-doers; renunciation of cyclic existence; and generation of the altruistic Mahāyāna mind to realize buddhahood, relieve the sufferings of beings, take on the sufferings of beings, and establish beings in happiness. This sutra is so extremely short, I simply translate it here as the easiest way to illustrate the ways in which it is different:

The Sutra on the Eight Realizations of Great Men
(T17.0779.715b)

Translated by the Parthian Tripiṭaka Master An Shigao (100?–170 CE)

This was spoken for the sake of the disciples of the Buddha. They were constant in their ultimately sincere recitation and remembrance, both day and night, of the eight realizations of great men.

First, one realizes:
That the world is impermanent;
That one's country is a fragile entity;
That the four great elements are freighted with suffering and are themselves empty;

That the five aggregates are devoid of self, that they are subject to change and transformation through production and destruction, and that they are empty, false, and devoid of any [inherently-existent subjective] agent.

That the mind is a source of evil and that one's physical form is like a thicket in which karmic offenses are created.

One carries on analytic contemplation in accordance with these factors and gradually abandons cyclic births and deaths.

Second, one realizes that an abundance of desire is the basis of suffering, that the laboriousness and weariness arising in the sphere of cyclic births and deaths arises from desire, and that it is in less desire and realization of the unconditioned that the body and mind experience sovereign independence.

Third, one realizes that the mind is insatiable and prone to ever greater seeking and to the proliferation of the evils associated with karmic offenses. The bodhisattva is not this way. He is constantly mindful in knowing when enough is enough. He establishes himself in circumstances akin to poverty, and guards [the practices which accord with] the Path, realizing that it is wisdom alone which constitutes the Path.

Fourth, one realizes that indolence is associated with falling [into unfortunate circumstances]. Thus one is constant in the practice of vigor and the destruction of the evils associated with the afflictions. One conquers the four demons [of the four great elements] and escapes from the prison of the aggregates and sense realms.

Fifth, one realizes the nature of delusion and cyclic births and deaths. The bodhisattva remains constantly mindful of this and, being broad-ranging in his studies, possesses much learning. He increases his wisdom, perfects eloquence, provides transformative teaching to everyone, and thereby brings great happiness to all.

Sixth, one realizes that poverty, suffering, and an abundance of adversaries makes for the sudden and tragic development of conditions associated with evil. Thus the bodhisattva practices giving and is equally mindful of both adversaries and close relations. He does not hold in mind evils from long ago, and does not detest people who are evil.

Seventh, one realizes the faults and disastrousness associated with the five desires. Even though one may still be a layperson, he does not allow himself to become defiled by worldly pleasures. He bears in mind those "vessels of Dharma" possessing the three robes and the bowl. He becomes determined to leave behind the home life and to guard [the practice of] the Path in pristine purity. Thus he becomes lofty and far-reaching in the brahman conduct (celibacy, etc.) and acts out of kindness and compassion for everyone.

Eighth, one realizes that cyclic births and deaths are as if ablaze and are connected with countless sufferings and afflictions. Thus one generates the mind associated with the Mahāyāna resolved to rescue everyone. He vows to substitute for beings in the taking on of their incalculably many sufferings and vows to cause all beings to develop the most ultimate form of great happiness.

Eight matters such as these are realized by all buddhas and bodhisattvas, those who are great men. They are vigorous in the practice of the Path and are imbued with kindness and compassion as they cultivate wisdom. They go aboard the ship of the Dharma body and thereby arrive at the shore of nirvāṇa. They then repeatedly return to the sphere of cyclic birth and death to bring about the liberation of beings.

They resort to the above eight matters in their instruction and guidance of everyone. Thus they influence beings to awaken to the sufferings of cyclic birth and death, influence them to abandon the five desires, and influence them to cultivate the mind's path of the Āryas.

If a disciple of the Buddha recites these eight topics, he thereby extinguishes countless karmic transgressions and advances along toward bodhi. He will swiftly ascend to the right enlightenment, thus eternally cutting off cyclic births and deaths and abiding forever in happiness.

End of *The Sutra on the Eight Realizations of Great Men*

---

123 – Cultivate Purification in the Five Types of Spiritual Abilities

The heavenly ear, the heavenly eye,
The bases of spiritual powers, the cognition of others' thoughts,
And the cognition of past lives and abodes—
One should cultivate purification of these five spiritual abilities.

■ (Bhikshu Vaśitva simply restates the *śloka's* obvious surface meaning and then introduces the ensuing text with the question: "How does one go about cultivating them?")

TN These powers may be realized as a consequence of past-life spiritual cultivation or as a consequence of present-life path practices such as *dhyāna* meditation. Such "powers" are not, in and of themselves, particularly desirable or useful unless counterbalanced by wisdom, this because of the inherent karmic hazards to both self and others in their misuse.

These dangers make cultivation and realization of Mahāyāna altruistic motivation (*bodhicitta*) and the four immeasurables more urgent. Why? They help insure the constant presence of that correct motivation which always bears in mind the spiritual welfare of others. If one *does* gain adequately counter-balancing wisdom together with well-developed integration of the four immeasurables, one may then skillfully use such powers in teaching. This is why Nāgārjuna makes the four immeasurables a primary topic in the very next *śloka*.

The cognition of another's thoughts, and the cognition of another's past lives are probably the two most useful of these spiritual "skills" in teaching others. This is because the knowledge which they allow one to access is especially helpful in the clear diagnosis of another's karmic circumstances. With the ability to clearly observe past lives and present thought-streams, one becomes better able to select the precisely appropriate teachings well tailored to the karmic needs of any given Dharma student.

---

124 – The Four Bases Are Their Root; the Four Immeasurables Govern Them

The four bases of spiritual powers comprise their root.
They are zeal, vigor, mental focus, and contemplative reflection.
The four immeasurables govern them.
They are kindness, compassion, sympathetic joy, and equanimity.

AV As cultivation of the four immeasurables deepens, the four dhyānas are realized in sequence along with physical and mental pliancy (*praśrabhi*), thus enabling access to the path of the super-knowledges (*abhijñā*). One then generates the bases of the spiritual powers (*ṛddhi pāda*), namely: "zeal" (*chanda*); "vigor" (*vīrya*); "[focused] thought" (*citta*); and contemplative reflection (*mīmāṃsā*).

The minds of those bodhisattvas abide in such sovereign mastery of these matters that, in all situations, they pursue their activities just as readily as wind is able to blows along freely through open space.

After those bodhisattvas have realized the four immeasurable minds and the four dhyānas, they develop the heavenly eye to an extent that its power becomes uniquely superior to that possessed by gods, dragons, *yakṣas*, *śrāvakas* or pratyekabuddhas. As they develop it, it becomes superior in terms of purity, illumination, primacy, and distinctiveness. It is unimpeded in its ability to observe all aspects of the world, whether coarse or subtle, far or near.

So too, they develop the heavenly ear's ability to hear the sounds of the gods, the humans, and the animals. So too, they develop the ability to have unbounded recall of [both their own and others'] previous existences. So too, they develop the ability to know the thoughts and motivations of others with a refinement capable of distinguishing countless variations. So too, they develop spiritual power so consummately that they are able to subdue whomever must be subdued.

TN Although Bhikshu Vaśitva implicitly describes how the generation of powers through cultivation of the four bases of spiritual powers flows forth from the four immeasurables, he does not really comment directly on Nāgārjuna's declaration that the four immeasurables (*apramāṇacitta*) "govern" the practices and spiritual powers mentioned immediately above. Nāgārjuna's intent in making the statement is worthy of our curiosity and warrants exploration.

The rationale for Nāgārjuna's statement regarding the "governance" function of the four immeasurables may be in large measure deduced simply through recalling the uses of the four immeasurables (For more on this, see my translation of *Nāgārjuna on the Four Immeasurable Minds*):

Kindness (*maitrī*) nurtures an affectionate mindfulness of beings, counters the development of hatred toward particularly unsavory classes of beings, and has as its motivation the desire to provide beings with happiness and security.

Compassion (*karuṇā*) causes one to bear in mind the physical and mental sufferings of beings, counters the development of any tendency to want to harm beings coursing in evil, and has as its motivation the wish to relieve suffering.

Sympathetic joy (*muditā*) nurtures a concordant celebration in the successes of beings, counters any tendency toward petty jealousies, and has as its motivation to cause beings to graduate from the mere experience of happiness to the ability to experience joyfulness.

Equanimity (*upekṣā*) allows one to relinquish any attachment to the goals involved in the first three of the four immeasurables even as one refuses to forsake the welfare of beings. The consequence of cultivating equanimity is an ability to abide in a state devoid of either aversion or affection. This is to a certain degree essential to a bodhisattva's ability to course on in the infinitely long practice of the Bodhisattva Path without succumbing to disappointment over the seeming futility of wishing to bestow happiness on all beings, to relieve the suffering of all beings, and to bring them all to a state of abundant joyfulness.

Finally, given the above, it should be obvious how the four immeasurables would counter any tendency toward arrogant misapplication of powers. It is in these senses then that one can understand Nāgārjuna's statement that the four immeasurables "govern" the spiritual powers.

---

125 – Regard Elements as Snakes, Senses as Empty Village, Aggregates as Assassins

The four elements are like poisonous serpents.
The six sense faculties are like an empty village.
The five aggregates are like assassins.
One should contemplate them in this way.

AV In spite of being guarded and carefully raised, the four elements of "earth" and such nonetheless move along precipitously [through disease, aging, and death]. Because they show no gratitude, can't be relied upon, and can't be trusted, they should be contemplated as like poisonous snakes.

Because they are devoid of any subjective agent and are unrelated to any self or possessions of a self, the sense faculties of the eye and so forth should be contemplated as like an empty village frequented by a band of six [sense-object] insurgents.

Because the five aggregates manifest as unitary phenomena through which one suffers destruction and punishment, one should contemplate them as like assassins.

TN Ārya Nāgārjuna narrates this scripture-based analogy more completely in his *Mahāprajñāpāramitā Upadeśa* (T25.1509.145b9–26). I quote it below from my translation of *Nāgārjuna on the Six Perfections*:

In the *Buddha Speaks the Analogy of the Poisonous Snakes Sutra,* there once was a man who had offended the King. The King ordered that he be required to carry around a basket and look after it. Inside the basket there were four poisonous snakes. The King ordered the criminal to look after them and raise them.

This man thought to himself, "It's a difficult thing to have to draw close to four snakes. If one grows close to them, they bring harm to a person. I could not raise even one of them, how much the less could I do that for four of them." And so he cast aside the basket and ran away.

The King ordered five men carrying knives to chase after him. There was yet another man who tried to persuade him to obey. [This other man] had it in mind to bring him harm and so said to him, "Just raise them in a sensible fashion. There will be no suffering in that." But the man became wise to this and so ran off, fleeing for his life. When he came to an empty village there was a good man who assisted him by telling him, "Although this village is empty, it is a place that is frequented by thieves. If you now take up residence here you will certainly be harmed by the thieves. Be careful. Don't dwell here."

At this point he took off again and next arrived at a great river. On the other side of the river there was a different country. That country was a peaceful, blissful, and easeful place. It was a pure place devoid of any form of calamity or adversity. Then he gathered together a mass of reeds and branches and bound them into the form of a raft. He moved it along with his hands and feet. He exerted all of his strength in seeking to make a crossing. When he had reached the other shore, he was at peace, happy, and free of distress.

The King represents the demon king. The basket represents the human body. The four poisonous snakes represent the four great elements. The five knife-wielding assassins represent the five aggregates. The man of fine speech but evil mind represents defiled attachment. The empty village represents the six sense faculties. The thieves represent the six sense objects. The one man who took pity on him and instructed him represents the good [spiritual] teacher. The great river represents love. The raft represents the eightfold right path. The hands and feet earnestly applied to making a crossing represent vigor. This shore represents this world. The far shore represents nirvāṇa. The man who crossed over represents the arhat who has put an end to outflow impurities. This is the same in the Dharma of the bodhisattva.

Those unfamiliar with the idea of "the four elements" of earth, water, fire, and air may find them conceptually confusing when they are stood alongside the western scientific "elements" most of us know from studying chemistry and physics. In fact, the concept is quite simple and easy to understand in scientific terms, as follows: The "four elements" of Indian Buddhist thought simply refer to the four elemental phases within which all manifest phenomena may be subsumed.

The four elements are not actually inherently-existent "fixed" categories reflecting an irreducible chemical nature as per the western scientific concept of "elements." In fact, it is common for the elements of western science to manifest, depending upon their temperature, as any of these four elemental phases referred to by Buddhists: as "earth" (i.e. "solidity," when at lower relative temperatures), as "water" (i.e. "liquidity," when heated to a relatively higher temperature), as "fire" (during combustion), and as "air" (i.e. "vaporousness," when forced by heat to enter a gaseous state).

Understanding this relationship between the two concepts of "elements" should make the nature of the Buddha's "four elements" obvious and conceptually agreeable, both as valid categories of epistemological observation and as important didactic concepts assisting understanding of the Path.

Now, having explored the concept of the four primary elements, it is worth noting that Nāgārjuna makes a point of utterly demolishing the idea that they might enjoy any degree of ultimate reality. An exemplary case may be found in the first chapter (*ślokas* 83–90) of the *Ratnāvalī*. See under separate cover my complete translation of that treatise's earliest extant version (approximately 550 CE, via Tripiṭaka Master Paramārtha).

It is precisely the mutability of the four elemental phases described by the Buddha which make them every bit as dangerous as carrying around a basket of venomous snakes which may bite and kill one at any time.

---

126 – Esteem Dharma and Its Teachers, Eschew Stinginess, Listen Closely to Dharma

Esteem the Dharma and the masters of Dharma
And also relinquish any stinginess with the Dharma.
The instructing masters must not be tight-fisted or secretive
And those listening must not be mentally scattered or confused.

AV There are four dharmas here capable of generating great wisdom. They are stating in essence that one must not entertain incorrect motivations.

---

127 – Speak Dharma, Free of Arrogance or Hopes, Motivated Solely by Compassion

Free of arrogance and free of hopes,
Motivated solely by thoughts of compassion and pity,
With reverent and respectful mind,
Expound the Dharma for the community.

AV There are four additional signs here of great wisdom which the bodhisattva should adopt:
  1) Abandonment of self-elevation and slighting of others through freedom from arrogance.
  2) Renunciation of any concern for offerings, reverence, or reputation through being free of any hopes.
  3) Feeling only compassion and pity due to being in the midst of beings hindered by the darkness of ignorance.
  4) Maintenance of a reverential and respectful frame of mind when explaining Dharma for the benefit of such beings.

---

128 – Be Insatiable in Learning, Don't Deceive the Venerables, Please Instructors

Be insatiable in learning
And always recite and retain what has been learned.
Do not deceive any among the venerable fields of merit.
Moreover, cause one's instructors to be delighted.

AV These are karmic causes for never forgetting the mind resolved on bodhi.

TN "Field of merit," is a specific reference to recipients of generosity which, through that act of giving, produce karmic merit for the benefactor. The Buddha, the Dharma, and the Ārya Sangha are the most obvious examples. In this context, the reference is specifically to monastic sangha members serving as teachers of Dharma.

The Buddha sought to illustrate this concept by ordering that the robes of monks and nuns be sewn in a patchwork pattern resembling the patch-work appearance of plots of cultivated farmland, this to illustrate that deeds done in support of monastics are karmically meritorious and are bound to bring definite karmic rewards.

When done, such deeds plant karmic "seeds" which sprout forth as positive karmic circumstances in the benefactor's future.

---

129 – Don't Pay Visits for Gifts or Respect, Don't Study Worldly Texts for Debate

One should not pay visits to the houses of others
With a mind cherishing reverence or offerings.
One must not take up study and recitation of worldly texts
For the sake of debating challenging topics.

AV One should not pay such visits except where that may facilitate someone's resolve to realize bodhi. One should not study such texts except where they facilitate broad-based learning.

---

130 – Don't Defame Bodhisattvas or Slander Dharmas Not Yet Understood

One must not be provoked by hatefulness or anger
Into defaming any bodhisattva.
As for dharmas not yet received or learned,
One must not initiate slanders in those cases either.

AV Why not? In order to preserve the continuous production of good dharmas.

---

131 – Sever Arrogance, Abide in the Lineage Bases, Avoid Disapproving, Halt Conceit

In order to cut off arrogance and pride,
One should abide in the four lineage bases of the ārya.
One must not course in disapproval of others
And must not allow oneself to become conceited.

AV Abide among beings with the mind "lowered" as one might were one but a dog, this to cut off self pride. Through the "four lineage bases of the ārya" one looks lightly on and tends toward frugality in matters having to do with robes, food, bedding and medicines, this because, in the lineage bases of the ārya, one is easily satisfied.

TN In fascicle twenty-seven of his commentary on the *Great Perfection of Wisdom Sutra* (*Mahāprajñāpāramitā Upadeśa*), Nāgārjuna lists the four lineage bases of the ārya (*āryavaṃśa*) as: "refraining from selective discrimination regarding robes, food, bedding and medicines, while delighting in cutting off suffering and cultivating meditative absorption." (T25.1509.258a19)

132 – Don't Expose Others' Offenses or Find Fault, Be Aware of One's Own Errors

Whether or not someone has actually committed a transgression,
One must not reveal his situation to others.
Do not seek out the errors and faults of anyone else.
Rather one should become aware of one's own errors.

AV Where someone committed to brahman conduct might have committed a karmic offense, no matter whether or not an offense was actually committed, one must never expose such situations.

TN "Brahman conduct" (*brahmacarya*) refers primarily to the absolute celibacy vow of a monk, nun, novice, or female monastic probationer, but also refers less directly to the other major monastic vows.

It may be worth noting here that neither Ārya Nāgārjuna nor Bhikshu Vaśitva are recommending either tolerating or covering up ethics violations in the Buddhist community. The Buddha laid down very clear methods for dealing with all such problems. Traditional Buddhist communities adhering to those protocols deal with these sorts of issues very efficiently and effectively.

133 – Avoid Criticism or Doubt Toward Buddha or Dharma, Keep Faith in the Abstruse

One should refrain from biased judgments and doubting
In fathoming the Buddha and the Dharma of the Buddhas.
Even though a dharma may be extremely difficult to believe,
One should nonetheless maintain faith in it.

AV Do not resort to discriminating thought or doubt-derived delusions as means to fathom either Buddha or Dharma, for these are matters beyond the ken of the common man and are dharmas not held in common with any other beings. Even for the most incredibly recondite dharmas, one should maintain pure faith arising from profound thought.

TN When Bhikshu Vaśitva mentions "dharmas not held in common with any other beings," he is directly referencing "the eighteen dharmas exclusive to the Buddhas" and indirectly referencing the ten powers, the four fearlessnesses, and the four unimpeded knowledges which, although shared to a greater or lesser degree by exalted beings such as arhats, pratyekabuddhas, and bodhisattvas, are unfamiliar territory for the common man. I list these thirty-six dharmas below as short selections I've drawn from my translations of the much longer discussions found in Ārya Nāgārjuna's commentary on the *Great Perfection of Wisdom Sutra*, this to make it obvious why Nāgārjuna would warn us: "One should refrain from using the discriminating mind and doubt in fathoming the Buddha and the Dharma of the Buddhas."

The Eighteen Dharmas Exclusive to Buddhas:

1) They are free of physical errors.
2) They are free of verbal errors.
3) They are free of errors in mindfulness.
4) They are free of discriminating thoughts.
5) They are free of unconcentrated thoughts.
6) They are free of equanimity deriving from incomplete awareness.
7) Their zeal is unfailing.
8) Their vigor is unfailing.
9) Their mindfulness is unfailing.
10) Their wisdom is unfailing.
11) Their liberations are unfailing.
12) Their knowledge and vision associated with the liberations are unfailing.
13) All of their physical actions accord with their prior cognition.
14) All of their verbal actions accord with their prior cognition.
15) All of their mental actions accord with their prior cognition.
16) They are unimpeded in their knowledge of the past.
17) They are unimpeded in their knowledge of the future.
18) They are unimpeded in their knowledge of the present.

The Ten Powers:

The first power is that he knows in accordance with actual truth what can be as what can be and what cannot be as what cannot be.

The second power is that he knows all of the karmic activity and all of the experiences of beings throughout past time, throughout future time, and in the present time, knows the location at which they created the karmic action, knows its associated causes and conditions, and knows the associated retribution.

The third power is that he knows all of the dhyānas,

liberations, samādhis, and absorptions and knows in accordance
with actual truth the distinctive characteristics defining their
relative defilement and purity.

The fourth power is that he knows all of the faculties
possessed by other beings and knows in accordance with actual
truth the characteristics by which they (the faculties) qualify as
superior or inferior.

The fifth power is that he knows all of the different sorts of
desires possessed by other beings.

The sixth power is that he knows all of the world's countless
categories of different natures.

The seventh power is that he knows the characteristic
features of the end point of all paths.

The eighth power is that he knows the various sorts of previous
lifetimes together with their commonly-held characteristics and
their commonly-held causes and conditions, knows them for
a single lifetime, for two lifetimes, and so forth until we come
to a hundred thousand lifetimes, knows them from the very
beginning of the kalpa on through to the very end of the kalpa,
and knows, "I possessed this surname and this given name as
I abided among those particular beings, consumed such-and-
such drink and food, and experienced such-and-such sufferings
and happinesses, and possessed a lifespan of such-and-such a
length. Having died among those beings, I was then reborn in
this place. Having died in this place, I returned to birth in this
place. And when I was born in this place, precisely this was my
surname, given name, the sorts of drink and food consumed,
the sufferings and happinesses experienced, and the length of
lifespan lived out."

The ninth power is that the Buddha's heavenly eye is purified
beyond that of the heavenly eye possessed by the gods. He sees
with that eye the time of beings' death, the time of their births,
the fineness and ugliness of their physical features, whether they
are great or small, whether they fall into the wretched destinies,
and whether they fall in among the wholesome destinies.

He sees that they undergo karmic retribution on account
of the causes and conditions associated with such-and-such
karmic activity, sees that the evil physical karmic activity of
these beings ripens completely, sees that their evil verbal karmic
activity ripens completely, and sees that their evil mental karmic
activity ripens completely.

He sees the erroneous views leading them to slander the

Āryas, sees that the karmic activity associated with those erroneous views ripens completely, and sees that, on account of these causes and conditions, when their physical body comes to ruin and dies, they then enter the wretched destinies wherein they are reborn in the hells.

He sees that the wholesome physical karmic activity of these beings ripens completely, sees that their wholesome verbal karmic activity ripens completely, sees that their wholesome mental karmic activity ripens completely, and sees that their refraining from slandering the Āryas, their correct views, and their karmic actions arising from correct views—these all ripen completely as well. He sees that, on account of these causes and conditions, when their physical body comes to ruin and dies, they then enter into the wholesome destinies and are reborn in the heavens.

The tenth power is that, because the Buddha has brought all outflow impurities to an end, he has achieved the liberation associated with the mind free of outflow impurities, has achieved the wisdom associated with the mind free of outflow impurities, and knows and recognizes for himself, in accordance with actual truth, that, with respect to the dharmas of the present, "My births are already ended, my observance of the prohibitions has already been accomplished, and all subsequent existence has been brought to an end."

The Four Fearlessnesses
(a.k.a. "The Four Grounds of Self-Confidence"):

The first fearlessness: The Buddha set forth the honest statement in which he claimed, "I am a person possessing right knowledge of all things. I do not see even the slightest sign that I should fear that any śramaṇa, brahman, god, *māra*, Brahmā, or member of any other group could rightfully state that I do not know these dharmas. Based on this, I have realized the security and fearlessness of one established in the position of the leader among the Āryas [and abide there] like the king of bulls. In the midst of the Great Assembly, I roar the lion's roar and set rolling the brahman wheel which no śramaṇa, brahman, god, *māra*, Brahmā, or member of any other group can rightfully set rolling. This is the first of the fearlessnesses.

The second fearlessness: The Buddha set forth the honest statement in which he claimed, "I have put an end to all outflow impurities. I do not see even the slightest sign that I should fear that any śramaṇa, brahman, god, *māra*, Brahmā, or member of any other group could rightfully state that I have not brought these outflow impurities to an end. Based on this, I have realized the security and fearlessness of one established in the position of the leader among the Āryas [and abide there] like the king of bulls. In the midst of the Great Assembly, I roar the lion's roar and set rolling the brahman wheel which no śramaṇa, brahman, god, *māra*, Brahmā, or member of any other group can rightfully set rolling. This is the second of the fearlessnesses.

The third fearlessness: The Buddha set forth the honest statement in which he claimed, "I have described the dharmas which constitute obstacles. I do not see even the slightest sign that I should fear that any śramaṇa, brahman, god, *māra*, Brahmā, or member of any other group could rightfully state that one may take on these obstructive dharmas and yet not find that they obstruct the Path. Based on this, I have realized the security and fearlessness of one established in the position of the leader among the Āryas [and abide there] like the king of bulls. In the midst of the Great Assembly, I roar the lion's roar and set rolling the brahman wheel which no śramaṇa, brahman, god, *māra*, Brahmā, or member of any other group can rightfully set rolling. This is the third of the fearlessnesses.

The fourth fearlessness: The Buddha set forth the honest statement in which he claimed, "The path of the Ārya which I have proclaimed is able to take one beyond the world. If one follows this path, one becomes able to put an end to all suffering. I do not see even the slightest sign that I should fear that any śramaṇa, brahman, god, *māra*, Brahmā, or member of any other group could rightfully state that, coursing in this path, one remains unable to go beyond the world and unable to put an end to suffering. Based on this, I have realized the security and fearlessness of one established in the position of the leader among the Āryas [and abide there] like the king of bulls. In the midst of the Great Assembly, I roar the lion's roar and set rolling the brahman wheel which no śramaṇa, brahman, god, *māra*, Brahmā, or member of any other group can rightfully set rolling. This is the fourth of the fearlessnesses.

The Four Unimpeded Knowledges:

The "four unimpeded knowledges" refer to unlimited ability to bring forth meanings, dharmas, language, and eloquence.

134 – Even Though One May Be Put to Death, One Should Still Speak Only the Truth

Even though one might be put to death for speaking the truth,
Or might be forced to abdicate the throne of a universal monarch,
Or even that of a king among the gods,
One should still utter only truthful speech.

AV How much the less might he fail to speak the truth in other circumstances.

135 – Even if Beaten, Cursed, or Terrorized, Don't Hate or Condemn; See It as Karma

Even if beaten, cursed, or terrorized with death threats or captivity,
One must not hate or condemn others, but should instead reflect:
"This is all the product of my own karmic offenses.
This has happened as a result of karmic retribution."

AV These events are a result of previous karmic offenses. Hence it is only fitting that such events now occur. Rather than nourishing hatred for the assailant, one should reflect: "This is just my karma. I already took part in such things in previous lifetimes. So now I undergo the identically undesirable karmic result. As a matter of fact, these assailants are actually free of any karmic offense in this."

136 – Support Parents Generously, Serve the Needs of Monastic Instructors as Well

One should, with the most ultimate respect and affection,
Provide offerings in support of one's father and mother.
Also supply the needs of and serve the *upādhyāyas*,
While extending reverence to the *ācāryas* as well.

AV No matter where they live, with the utmost affection and respect, provide offerings to support parents. Look upon them as deities, adapt to their wishes to cause them to be pleased, and abandon any flattery or deceptiveness in relations with them.

Also revere and supply the needs of the *upādhyāyas* and *ācāryas*, while also according with their instructions to remain free of inward secrecy and devote oneself instead to instructing others.

TN *Upādhyāyas* are monastic preceptors and instructors of slightly lesser station, whereas the *ācāryas* are those who discharge the highest monastic teaching and precept-transmittal responsibilities.

---

137 – Discoursing on Profound Dharmas for Two-Vehicles Practitioners Is an Error

When, for those who place their faith in the Śrāvaka Vehicle
Or those dedicated to the Pratyekabuddha Vehicle,
One discourses on the most profound of dharmas,
This, for a bodhisattva, is an error.

AV Starting here, we have four types of bodhisattva practice errors which should be abandoned by the bodhisattva.

TN By "the most profound of dharmas," Nāgārjuna would likely include any of the Great Vehicle teachings which would not be readily understood and believed by an audience dedicated to rapid acquisition of the individual-liberation paths culminating in arhatship or pratyekabuddhahood. For example, we have:

1)   Not just the emptiness of persons which is already available in those traditions (but potentially problematic for a lay audience), but rather also: "the emptiness of dharmas" (and its implications for understanding and practice).

2)   The identity of nirvāṇa and saṃsāra (cyclic existence).

3)   The identity of afflictions (*kleśas*) and bodhi (the danger being here that a shocked audience might misconstrue this to imply endorsement of affliction-ridden karma).

4)   The great kindness and compassion of the bodhisattva (as distinct from the mere mind-conditioning contemplation of kindness and compassion as affliction-countering stances, this latter being what is typical in Two-Vehicles' *brahma-vihāra* practice).

5)   The three great asaṃkhyeya eons of practice required to perfect the causes of buddhahood, including the willingness to enter even the hells to pursue the Bodhisattva Path.

Teaching such dharmas to a Two-Vehicles audience poses two obvious dangers:

1)   They might well be moved to slander Great-Vehicle teachings, thus doing themselves unnecessary but very serious karmic harm.

2)   They could well find that their faith in the Śrāvaka Vehicle is undermined while they are as yet unable to develop deep faith in the Great Vehicle. This then could result in their falling away from all Buddhist paths to liberation.

For an audience of this sort, it is probably best to focus primarily on concepts and practices associated with the four truths of the

Ārya, the eight-fold path, the thirty-seven wings of enlightenment, the twelve links of conditioned arising, or correct practice of calming-and-contemplation (*śamatha-vipaśyanā*) meditation.

---

138 – Discoursing on Two-Vehicles Tenets to the Great-Vehicle Faithful is an Error

When, for believers in the profound Great Vehicle teachings,
One discourses to those beings
On the Śrāvaka or Pratyekabuddha vehicles,
This too is an error for him.

AV (Simply restates very briefly the *śloka's* surface meaning.)

TN The problem with discoursing on Śrāvaka-Vehicle doctrine to a Mahāyāna audience is that those who have nominally dedicated themselves to the Bodhisattva Path but have not yet gained irreversible advancement in it may be moved to turn back to the individual-liberation path of the Śrāvaka Vehicle. In effect, they could thereby cheat themselves out of buddhahood while also cheating countless beings out of liberation whom they would otherwise have been able to bring across to liberation as they coursed along on the Bodhisattva Path.

---

139 – The Two Other Errors: Failing to Teach the Worthy, Trusting Wrongdoers

So too where some superior person comes seeking the Dharma,
But one delays and fails to provide him with teachings.
So too where, on the contrary, one takes in wrongdoers
Or delegates responsibilities to those who are untrustworthy.

AV When an upstanding superior person comes requesting instruction, one should immediately discourse on good dharmas for his benefit. In this case, one fails to do so and, beyond that, delays.

When a person comes who is a transgressor against the moral precepts and one takes just the opposite course of action by taking them in and trusting them even though they as yet have no faith or understanding of the Great Vehicle, this is a bodhisattva practice error.

TN This same list of "four bodhisattva errors" is also found in Nāgārjuna's *Ten Grounds Vibhāṣā*. There, briefly commenting on his *śloka* line, "The bodhisattva should abandon the four types of bodhisattva errors," Nāgārjuna explains them as follows:

"What are 'the four types of [bodhisattva] errors'?:

1) Where one discourses on extremely recondite dharmas for beings who are not vessels [appropriate for such teaching], this is an error.

2) Where one discourses on the Small Vehicle for those who delight in recondite, vast-scope dharmas, this is an error.

3) Where one is slightingly arrogant and disrespectful toward someone who engages in correct practice of the Path, is a holder of precepts, and who has a wholesome mind, this is an error.

4) Where we have someone who has not yet developed and has not yet become trustworthy, and yet one places trust in him—where one takes in an evil man who is a breaker of precepts, taking him to be a friend and someone who is good, this is an error." (十住毘婆沙論 / T26.1521.66b–c)

---

140 – Abandon These Errors While Also Studying and Adopting the *Dhūta* Practices

One must abandon the errors mentioned above.
As for such herein-described meritorious practices as the *dhūtas*,
One ought to become knowledgeable about them
And then incorporate them into one's own practice.

AV The four earlier-described errors must be abandoned as they stray far from bodhi. As for the previously-mentioned Śrāvaka and Pratyekabuddha vehicles practices, including the *dhūta* (ascetic) practices, learn about them and adopt them in practice.

TN So long as one maintains strong resolve focused on highest bodhi, those fundamental doctrines and practice methods often more directly associated with the arhat or pratyekabuddha path may be viewed and *should* be viewed as essential foundational training for the bodhisattva practitioner. This is why Nāgārjuna makes a point of bringing up this matter repeatedly in this and other treatises.

---

141 – Maintain Four Types of Uniformly Equal Bodhisattva Path Practices

Regard all equally in one's thoughts, speak equally for all,
Be uniformly equal in establishing all others in goodness,
And influence them all equally to accord with what is right.
Thus one refrains from making distinctions between any beings.

AV These are four types of bodhisattva path practices to be adopted:

1) Uniform equality in thought raised toward all other beings.

2) Uniform equality in discoursing on Dharma for all beings.

3) Uniform equality in establishing all beings in goodness.

4) [Uniform equality] in influencing all beings to act in accordance with what is right.

In all such endeavors, one avoids making discriminating distinctions between beings.

TN Although the order of presentation differs in the commentary (numbers two and three are switched), this same list of four bodhisattva path practices is also found in Nāgārjuna's *Ten Grounds Vibhāṣā*. Because Dharmagupta's rendering is ambiguous, I present a translation of Nāgārjuna himself to corroborate the validity of this English rendering of Dharmagupta. Briefly commenting on his *śloka* line, "The bodhisattva should cultivate the four types of bodhisattva path practices," Nāgārjuna explains as follows:

> What are "the four types of bodhisattva path practices"?
>
> 1) One courses in uniformly equal thought toward all beings.
>
> 2) One instructs them all in the dharmas of goodness.
>
> 3) One discourses on Dharma equally for all beings.
>
> 4) One adopts the practice of right conduct [as a teaching] for all beings." (十住毘婆沙論 / T26.1521.66b–c)

For those who might find it useful, I briefly discuss and distinguish these ideas below:

1) "Uniform equality of thought" would require, for instance, that one consider a being coursing in evil no less worthy of kindness and compassionate concern than a person coursing in goodness.

2) "Uniform equality in discoursing on Dharma for all beings" would require, for instance, that, though the dharmas chosen in teaching would necessarily differ for the morally dissolute and those with refined spiritual sensibilities, they would both be deemed equally worthy of instruction in Dharma.

3) As for "establishing all beings in goodness," what comprises "goodness" in this context is defined by the path of the ten good karmic deeds (restraint from killing, stealing, sexual misconduct,

lying, harsh speech, divisive speech, frivolous or lewd speech, covetousness, hatefulness, wrong views).

4) As for "influencing all beings to act in accordance with what is right," what is right in this context is defined by the degree to which any given act of body, mouth, or mind aligns itself with wisdom.

---

142 – One Works for Dharma Over Benefit, Good Over Fame, Beings Over Happiness

One works for the sake of Dharma and not for self-benefit.
One works to develop meritorious qualities, not for renown.
One wishes to liberate beings from suffering
And does not wish merely to ensure his own happiness.

AV This *śloka* and the next deal with the four types of genuine bodhisattvas:

1) Those who work only for Dharma and not material benefit.

2) Those who work only to develop qualities, not fame.

3) Those who aspire only to liberate beings from suffering, not simply to ensure their own personal happiness.

(See next *śloka* for the fourth type of genuine bodhisattva.)

---

143 – One Works in Secret for the Many and so Relinquishes Personal Concerns

With purposes kept secret, one seeks fruition in one's works.
When the results of one's merit-generating endeavors come forth,
Even then, one applies them to the ripening of the many
While abandoning preoccupation with one's own concerns.

AV The fourth of the genuine bodhisattvas:

4) He keeps his intentions secret as he works to bring his karmic works to fruition, aided by practices which generate merit. When that merit manifests, he dedicates it to bodhi along with its abilities to benefit other beings and the many. Because his devotion is to the many, he relinquishes preoccupation with his own concerns.

TN This is another case where Nāgārjuna is directly referencing a section from his *Ten Grounds Vibhāṣā*, this time speaking of "four kinds of genuine bodhisattvas" which are the opposite of "the four kinds of counterfeit bodhisattvas" also discussed in that other treatise. I quote below the passage where he comments on his *śloka* line which says, "In the Dharma of the Bodhisattvas, there are four kinds of counterfeit bodhisattvas":

"What are 'the four [kinds of counterfeit bodhisattvas]'? They are:

1) He covets offerings and does not esteem the Dharma.

2) He devotes his efforts solely to gaining a reputation and does not seek to develop meritorious qualities.

3) He seeks to ensure his own happiness and so pays no mind to the plight of other beings.

4) He covets and finds pleasure in a personal retinue and so finds no happiness in renunciative solitude." (十住毘婆沙論 / T26.1521.66c)

It is easy to see how this list of "four types of genuine bodhisattvas" is simply the opposite of Nāgārjuna's "four types of counterfeit bodhisattvas" also described in the *Ten Grounds Vibhāṣā*. Perhaps the least obvious case is the fourth wherein the genuine bodhisattva, rather than cultivating a retinue, renounces all of that in favor of working secretly at perfecting the karma of the Bodhisattva Path, dedicating all of that merit to the welfare of other beings.

---

144 – Grow Close to the Four Types of Good Spiritual Friends

Grow close to good spiritual friends,
Specifically, to the masters of Dharma, to the Buddhas,
To those who encourage one to leave the home life,
And to those who are seekers of alms.

AV These are four categories of individuals serving as "good spiritual friends" (*kalyāṇamitra*) for the bodhisattva. One should grow close to them. What are the four categories? This refers to:

1)   The Dharma masters are good spiritual friends by assisting in developing wisdom arising from learning.

2)   The Buddhas, the Bhagavāns, serve as good spiritual friends by assisting in preserving the Dharma of all Buddhas.

3)   Those encouraging abandonment of home life serve as good spiritual friends by assisting in maintaining roots of goodness.

4)   Those who seek alms serve as good spiritual friends by assisting in maintaining the [altruistic] mind resolved on bodhi.

TN In the traditional context "masters of Dharma" is a specific reference to learned monks discoursing on Buddhist teachings.

In his *Ten Grounds Vibhāṣā*, Nāgārjuna, commenting on this very list, adds:

"The bodhisattva who cherishes *anuttara-samyak-saṃbodhi* (the utmost, right, and perfect enlightenment) should draw close to, revere, and make offerings to four kinds of good spiritual friends and should withdraw far from four kinds of bad spiritual friends." (十住毘婆沙論 / T26.1521.66c)

---

145 – Lokāyatas, Wealth Obsessives, Pratyekabuddha and Śrāvaka Vehicles Advocates

Those who ground themselves in worldly treatises,
Those who exclusively seek worldly wealth,
Those with Pratyekabuddha Vehicle faith and understanding,
And those devoted to the Śrāvaka Vehicle—

AV These four would be bad spiritual friends for bodhisattvas:

1) Those grounded in worldly treatises, this because they are devoted to clever rhetoric on various worldly topics.

2) Those focusing on accumulating wealth, this because they do not focus on Dharma.

3) Those advocating the Pratyekabuddha Vehicle, this because they are deficient in meaning-based benefit and good works.

4) Those advocating the Śrāvaka Vehicle, this because their practice is devoted primarily to self-benefit.

TN There is no intention on the part of either Nāgārjuna or Bhikshu Vaśitva to cast aspersions on the refined moral qualities of these last two profiles. Although they advocate valid Buddhist individual-liberation paths taught by the Buddha himself, they would still be unsuitable as companions for a bodhisattva because the inadequately-altruistic nature of their practice could exert a corrosive effect upon the determination of the bodhisattva practitioner.

Nāgārjuna's treatment of this list in his *Ten Grounds Vibhāṣā* specifically refers to "the non-Buddhist Lokāyatas," whereas Dharmagupta translated it more generically as "those grounded in worldly treatises." (十住毘婆沙論 / T26.1521.67a)

---

146 – Be Aware of Them As Unfit Spiritual Friends, Seek Out the Four Vast Treasuries

As for these four types of bad spiritual friends,
The bodhisattva should be aware of them as such.
There are, however, other circumstances one should seek out.
This refers specifically to the four vast treasuries:

AV These four would function as bad spiritual friends [for the bodhisattva practitioner]. One should withdraw [from taking them on as spiritual companions].

———

TN Nāgārjuna states in his *Ten Grounds Vibhāṣā*:

"Therefore the bodhisattva should draw near to the four kinds of good spiritual friends and withdraw from the four kinds of bad spiritual friends. If the bodhisattva is able to withdraw from the four kinds of bad spiritual friends and draw near to the four kinds of good spiritual friends, then he will be able to gain four vast treasuries and will be able to step beyond all dharmas linked to demon-related matters. He will be able to generate an immeasurable amount of merit and will be able to exhaustively accumulate all good dharmas." (十住毘婆沙論 / T26.1521.67a)

See the next *śloka* for the listing of these "four vast treasuries."

---

147 – Meeting Buddhas, Perfections Teachings, Dharma Masters, Solitary Practice

The emergence of buddhas; hearing the perfections explained;
Being able in the presence of a master of Dharma
To behold him with unobstructed mind;
And happily pursuing cultivation in a place of solitude.

AV Strive to obtain these four vast bodhisattva treasuries:

1) Serving the Buddhas when they come forth into the world.
2) Listening to explanations of the six pāramitās.
3) Beholding a master of the Dharma with unobstructed mind.
4) Practicing happily in solitude, free of neglectfulness.

———

TN In Nāgārjuna's comments on this list in his *Ten Grounds Vibhāṣā*, one discovers a few clarifying details:

"Bodhisattvas have four vast treasuries of sublime Dharma….

The third is that one's mind remains free of the obstacle of anger felt toward one who teaches the Dharma.

The fourth is that one's mind does not become neglectful as one happily abides in an *araṇya* (i.e. in an isolated meditation hermitage)." (十住毘婆沙論 / T26.1521.67a)

---

148 – Abide Like the Elements, Uniformly Equal in Benefiting All

Abide in a manner comparable to
Earth, water, fire, wind, and space,
Remaining thus uniformly equal under all circumstances
In providing benefit to all beings.

AV The element-like qualities which the bodhisattva should integrate are uniformly equal availability and beneficence.

For example, these elements don't manifest differently for different sentient or insentient things in which they are found useful. Thus all beings always remain able to put them to use without the elements changing in character or availability and without their seeking some reward in return for that.

One reflects, "I should emulate that even up till buddhahood."

---

149 – Reflect on Meanings, Progress in Uses of *Dhāraṇīs*, Don't Block Dharma Study

One should skillfully reflect upon the meanings
And diligently progress in the uses of the *dhāraṇīs*.
One must never create any sort of obstruction
To those seeking to hear the Dharma.

AV Skillfully reflect on the meanings of Buddha's teachings through discussion or contemplation.

Abide in mental purity through moral precepts. Stay diligent and immaculate in this while developing one's use of *dhāraṇīs*, in particular those such as the "Silver Lord" and "Ocean Lord."

Also, never create the slightest interference to anyone's intent to listen to Dharma teachings, this to avoid disastrous future karma.

TN The deep quietude of mind required for meditation practice or *dhāraṇī* practice is impossible to develop or maintain in the absence of the mental purity instilled by observance of moral precepts, hence Bhikshu Vaśitva's emphasis on the issue here.

The "Silver Lord" *dhāraṇī* mentioned by Bhikshu Vaśitva is still extant approximately 1500 years after its Sui Dynasty translation as the main topic of Chapter Eleven of the "Composite Edition" *Golden Light Sutra* (T16.664.386b05-11). I've so far been unable to locate the "Ocean Lord" *dhāraṇī*. Because *dhāraṇīs* often have several alternate names, it too could still be extant, just unrecognized for the time being.

Nāgārjuna discourses at length on *dhāraṇīs* in his commentary on the *Great Perfection of Wisdom Sutra*, most specifically in fascicle six and fascicle eight. Although I have translated all of that material, it is too long for inclusion here. Hence I simply present a detailed synopsis of the nature and uses of *dhāraṇīs* immediately below:

Dhāraṇīs are dharmas developed through spiritual cultivation by which one: a) retains good dharmas; b) blocks the arising of bad dharmas, and c) protects oneself from interference from negative spiritual forces which would otherwise destroy progress on the path of liberation.

In the popular imagination, *dhāraṇīs* are most usually associated with mantras (spiritually potent incantatory formulae), but that is not an entirely accurate perception, this because *dhāraṇīs* may in many instances be more closely identified with samādhis (deep meditative absorption states having very specific qualities and uses) or in come cases may not be particularly strongly associated with either mantras or samādhis.

I cite here a few examples of the "preservation," "suppression," and "protection" functions of *dhāraṇīs*:

a) Examples of good dharmas preserved by *dhāraṇīs* not just across the course of years, but also across the course of many lifetimes: karmic merit; moral precepts; specific well-developed meditation abilities; vows to continually pursue particular bodhisattva deeds.

b) Examples of bad dharmas, the arising of which may be spontaneously suppressed through well-matured practice of *dhāraṇīs*: negative karmic propensities originating with patterned negativity in the past; the arising of lust, hatred, delusion, or arrogance in response to objective circumstances in the present; the ability to formulate and carry through misguided or evil ideas such as hunting, drug-use, hate-speech, elective office for fame-and-profit, and so forth.

c) Examples of "negative spiritual forces" which may be countered through well-matured practice of *dhāraṇīs*: organized crime; charismatic cult leaders motivated by avarice for power, money or sex; powerfully negative mantras used by others for evil purposes; ghosts; demons; thieves; physical attackers.

Finally, a note of caution: Use of *dhāraṇīs* for other than the highest spiritual purposes is bound to be karmically disastrous. It is to be avoided at all costs.

150 – Overcome Major Afflictions, Banish Subsidiary Afflictions, Cast off Indolence

When embroiled in the afflictions, be able to overcome them.
Relinquish the lesser instances, retaining not a trace.
Regarding the eight cases involving indolence,
One should cut all of those off as well.

AV Through exercising self-control, overcome the [six primary] afflictions (covetousness, hatred, delusion, arrogance, doubtfulness, wrong views) arising in nine circumstances:

[1–3] Past, present, or future cases "not beneficial to me."

[4–6] Past, present, or future cases "not beneficial to dear ones."

[7–9] Past, present, or future cases "beneficial to those I detest."

Utterly relinquish the twenty subsidiary afflictions, namely: absence of faith; absence of a sense of shame, flattery, deceptiveness, agitation, mental scatteredness, negligence, harming, absence of a dread of blame, indolence, worry, drowsiness, enmity, concealment, jealously, miserliness, elevating oneself, anger, regretfulness, and depression.

Martial vigor to cut off indolence in eight typical cases:

[1] One thinks, "I'm about to take up a task," abandons vigor, and immediately lies down for a preparatory nap.

[2] One thinks, "I've now finished that task," or [3] "I've been walking along," or [4] "I'm all through with my walking," or [5] "My body is weary," and decides he can't do his cultivation work.

[6] Or else one thinks, "My body feels so heavy" [from eating too much] and then concludes he cannot do his cultivation work.

Or else one thinks, [7] "I've fallen ill," or [8] "My sickness has not yet subsided for very long," and then one immediately lies down peacefully, failing to generate any vigor.

Due to such circumstances, one doesn't achieve what should be achieved, doesn't arrive where he should arrive, and doesn't bring to realization what one should bring to realization.

151 – Don't Covet What Is Not One's Lot, Reconcile the Estranged

Do not covet what is not one's lot,
For unprincipled covetousness will not bring satisfaction.
Influence all who have become estranged to reconcile,
Whether or not they are one's own relations.

AV Where one observes others gaining abundant offerings, fame, happiness, esteem, and bounteous merit, refrain from thoughts covetous of what is not one's own lot. If one covets what is not one's own lot, one will fail to develop a satisfied mind.

Additionally, ignoring the question of whether or not they are one's own relatives, facilitate the reconciliation of all who have become involved in disputes, estrangement, and destructiveness. Influence the parties to restore that harmonious unity wherein they are agreeable and inclined to treat each other with kindness.

---

152 – Seeking to Get at Emptiness Itself Is Worse Than Viewing Body As Self

The wise must not base their practice
On getting at the "emptiness" in what is intrinsically empty.
In the case of one determined to get at that emptiness itself,
That wrong is even more extreme than viewing the body as a self.

AV Realization of emptiness is used to eliminate the mass of false conceptions arising from deficient wisdom. The wise must not take getting at emptiness itself as a practice goal, for that error [which attempts to make emptiness itself into some searchable entity] is even more extreme than that difficult-to-cure misconception which seizes on the body as constituting a self.

Attempting to seize on emptiness itself is an incurable metaphysical disease, for there is nothing above and beyond that to which one might resort to bring about a cure.

TN "Emptiness" is not a thing in itself. It is simply an absence of something. And of precisely what is it an absence? It is an absence of any inherent existence of some supposedly real entity over and above the mere assemblage of conditions composing any given phenomenon. That conception of some supposedly existent entity is really just an idea associated with a mere name, period.

For instance: A "car" doesn't have any inherent existence of its own above and beyond being just a simple temporary collection of metal, rubber, glass, paint, and so forth upon which we have psychically stamped the label "car" in an act of deluded imputation. Realizing the emptiness of inherent existence of some supposedly real entity we associate with the name "car" is simply recognizing this fact. There isn't actually any "emptiness" above and beyond that.

Hence there is no "entity" called "emptiness" which one might somehow be able to lay hold of through some yet more refined act of enlightened perception. The inference of the text is that to imagine such a thing and then tenaciously cling to such a concept is really a type of metaphysical pathology worse even than thinking of the body as constituting a "self."

---

153 – Maintain Stupas, Provide Adornments, and Make Offerings at the Stupas

By sweeping and finishing floors, by providing adornments,
By furnishing many varieties of drums and music,
And by offering fragrances, flower garlands, and other gifts,
Contribute offerings to the *caityas*.

AV Keep the *caitya* floors swept and coated while also providing fragrant garlands, burnable and powdered incenses, floral canopies, banners, and other articles of adornment and offering. Make such offerings to gain [in future rebirths] a fine and upright physical form, the fragrance of moral virtue, and sovereign freedoms.

Offerings of all different sorts of drums and music—wind instruments made from shells, stringed instruments, the waist-mounted drums, the large drums, the thundering drums, the clapping of hands [along with the rhythm], and so forth—this is done for the sake of gaining the heavenly ear.

---

154 – Provide Lantern Wheels, Stupa Canopies, Sandals, Carriages, Sedan Chairs

Create all sorts of lantern wheels
As offerings to the *caityas* and their buildings.
Provide canopies as well as sandals,
Horse-drawn carriages, sedan chairs, and the like.

AV In the *caitya* buildings, create fragrant-oil and ghee lanterns with garlands as offerings creating causes for the buddha eye.

Give parasols, canopies, sandals, carriages, sedan chairs, and so forth as causes for the bodhisattva's spiritual powers and path.

TN One might well wonder what is meant by a "lantern wheel," a type of offering seemingly not much present in modern Buddhist practice. Apparently it is a circular arrangement of lanterns set up and lit as an offering. There is a description in the Tripiṭaka of an offering of a "lantern wheel" inspired by a monk from India, this

occurring in China during the Tang Dynasty and witnessed by the
emperor from atop a city gate.

The lamp reached to a height of some two hundred feet (lit.
"twenty *zhang*") and involved the lighting of five hundred lanterns
made from gold and silver. Its appearance is described has having
been "like a flowering tree."

This occurred at the very dawn of the eighth century, during the
height of Buddhism's flourishing in China, by coincidence in the
year Bodhiruci completed the new translation of the *Accumulation
of Jewels Sutra* and in the same year that the famous *Avataṃsaka
Sutra* patriarch, Fazang, passed away (712 CE).

Although the precise shape is not described, the name suggests
that the pattern of lantern arrangement may well have been in the
design of the eight-spoked wheel of Dharma emblematic of the
eight-fold Path. (佛祖統紀 / T49.2035.373a)

---

155 – Find Happiness in Listening to Dharma, in Faith in Buddha, in Serving Sangha

One should especially find delight in the Dharma
And be happy knowing what is gained through faith in Buddha.
Delight in providing for and serving the monastic Sangha,
While also finding happiness through listening to right Dharma.

AV Delight in the Dharma and not solely in the karmic blessings
and pleasures of the five sorts of desire.

One should realize the benefits gained through faith in the
Buddha and not anchor trust and happiness solely in seeing his
form body.

Delight in providing for and serving the Sangha order, while not
delighting only in audiences and the protocols of greeting.

One should experience delight in listening to their teaching of
Dharma and never become self-satisfied that one has had enough
of that. One must not settle for the happiness arising from listening
to a few of their passing words.

---

156 – Dharmas Don't Arise in the Past, Abide in the Present, or Extend into the Future

They do not arise in the past.
They do not abide in the present.
They do not go forward into the future.
Contemplate all dharmas in this manner.

AV Phenomena aren't produced in the past because: a) their existence is solely a function of the coinciding of subsidiary causes and conditions, and b) they have no place from whence they come.

Phenomena do not dwell in the present because: a) they are undergoing continuous [and complete] destruction in each successive micro-moment (*kṣaṇa*), and b) they consequently never abide at all.

Phenomena do not proceed on forward into the future because: a) they are undergoing such complete [and continuous micro-moment–to–micro-moment] destruction that no trace of them remains, and b) they have no place to which they go.

One should direct such analytic contemplation to all dharmas.

---

157 – Bestow What Is Best, Seek No Reward, Take on Sufferings, Do Not Covet Bliss

Give to beings whatsoever is fine
And do not wish that they bestow anything fine in return.
One should prefer it be solely oneself who endures suffering
While not favoring oneself in the enjoyment of happiness.

AV Give what is best to provide happiness for beings without seeking any commensurate reward. Be willing to endure countless sufferings on others' behalf. Nourish the thought that one's own happiness-facilitating possessions should be bestowed on beings for their enjoyment.

---

158 – Don't Be Overjoyed at Karmic Rewards Nor Downcast at Karmic Misfortune

Although replete with karmic rewards from immense merit,
The mind should not become lofty or overwhelmed with delight.
Although one may be as poverty-stricken as a hungry ghost,
One should still not become downcast or overcome with distress.

AV Even though one might have fallen into the extreme poverty, disastrous misfortune, and torment of a hungry ghost's extremely difficult life, one should still not become downcast or overcome with anguish. How much the less should one allow this to occur when, still abiding in the human realm, one falls into poverty and experiences disastrous misfortune.

159 – Esteem the Learned, Inspire the Untrained to Study Without Belittling Them

Accord the most ultimate degree of esteem
To those already accomplished in learning.
Inspire those as yet unlearned to devote themselves to study.
One should not behave in a manner belittling them.

AV (Simply restates surface meaning.)

TN By "those already accomplished in learning," Nāgārjuna would not be referring to those solely in command of a sea of Dharma "facts." Rather he would intend to reference those whose wisdom and practice of the Path have become well developed through wide-ranging study and integration of Dharma teachings.

Slighting beginning students of Dharma tends to beget future-life negative karmic consequences such as: dull-wittedness, inability to encounter right Dharma, inability to find and recognize a genuinely good guru, low social station, and being constantly mocked by others.

160 – Revere Virtue, Inspire Purity, Draw Close to the Wise, Promote Wisdom in Fools

Revere those perfect in observance of the moral precepts
And influence those who break precepts to take on the precepts.
Draw close to those perfect in wisdom
And influence those who act foolishly to abide in wisdom.

AV Press palms together and revere those perfect in observing the precepts, praising the karmic merit inhering in moral virtue.

On meeting those who break precepts, inspire them to take on the precepts, describing the retributions for breaking precepts.

Draw close to the wise, speaking in a manner describing the fine qualities accruing to those coursing in wisdom.

Influence the foolish to course in wisdom, discoursing for them on the faults inherent in foolish actions.

161 – Don't Be Terrorized by Saṃsāra, Rather Subdue Demons and Evil Knowledge

The sufferings of cyclic existence are of many kinds,
Involving birth, aging, death, and the wretched destinies.
One should not be frightened by the fearsomeness of these.
One must instead subdue demons and knowledge rooted in evil.

AV Whilst coursing along in cyclic births and deaths, the bodhisattva undergoes many kinds of sufferings such as birth, aging, death, lamentation, suffering-inducing afflictions, and the wretched destinies of the hells, animals, hungry ghosts, and *asuras* (demi-gods). One should not fear those things, but rather should focus only on subduing evil demons and those types of knowledge which are rooted in evil.

TN "Demons" are of many sorts. They include:

1) The demons of one's own mind (path-eroding thought patterns, etc.).

2) The demons of afflictions (desire, hatred, delusion, arrogance, doubt, wrong views, etc.).

3) Mischievous ghosts.

4) Sixth desire heaven deities.

5) Also, figuratively speaking, unwholesome acquaintances devoid of ethics or spiritual interests who, intentionally or not, subtly undermine one's faith and practice.

"Knowledge rooted in evil" is a reference to whichever forms of either esoteric or mundane knowledge may influence one to deviate from right-Dharma Path practice in favor of pursuing objects of the desires (wealth, sex, fame, etc.).

As for "subduing demons," helpful prophylactic and counteractive stratagems in dealing with demons include:

1) Deeply sincere daily repentance purifications, even if only as brief reflections at the altar.

2) Daily refreshing of the three refuges and at least the four basic bodhisattva vows, even if only as brief reflections at the altar.

3) Prayers to buddhas and bodhisattvas for their assistance.

4) Mantras invoking the protective assistance of Dharma-protecting spirits.

5) Constant purity in upholding the moral precepts.

6) Intensely diligent dedication to meritorious works.

7) Avoidance of involvement in worldly entertainments and pastimes.

As noted earlier in these notes, Dhyāna Master Zhiyi devotes an entire chapter to the issue of demons, demonic karma, how they manifest, and how their influences may be countered in his *Essentials for Practicing Calming-and-Insight and Dhyāna Meditation*. I have translated that entire work and am publishing it separately under the title *The Essentials of Buddhist Meditation*.

---

162 – Amass Merit in All Buddhalands, Make Vows That Others Will Reach Them Too

Amass every form of merit
In the lands of all the Buddhas.
Bring forth vows and proceed with vigor
So that everyone may succeed in reaching them.

AV Amass superior forms of merit in the lands of all buddhas in the ten directions by assisting in the perfection and adornment of those lands, by hearing teachings from buddhas and bodhisattvas, and by developing the ability to see them directly.

All of this is dedicated to causing all beings to be able to arrive in their own buddhaland. Make vows according with this intent. Whatever one vows to do, one proceeds immediately to accomplish that. In this too, one should proceed accordingly, availing oneself of intense diligence as one proceeds in cultivation.

---

163 – Never Seize on Dharmas, Abide in Equanimity, Take Up the Burden for Beings

Even in the midst of all dharmas, one is constant
In not seizing on them, thus coursing along in equanimity.
One takes on the burden, wishing to bear it on forth,
Proceeding in this manner for the sake of all beings.

AV It is through grasping that one suffers and through refraining from grasping that one enjoys happiness. On realizing this, one is constant in desisting from seizing on any phenomenon and so abides in equanimity.

Even so, having earlier made the vow to assist beings in reaching enlightenment, one is now willing to take up this burden for beings, wishing to carry it on forth.

---

164 – Contemplate Dharmas as Non-Self, Don't Relinquish Compassion or Kindness

Abide in the right contemplation of all dharmas
As devoid of self and as devoid of anything belonging to a self.
Even so, one must not relinquish the great compassion
Or one's reliance on the great kindness.

AV It is because they are like a dream and like a magical conjuration that dharmas are said to be devoid of self.

As for their being devoid of anything belonging to a self, this is based on the contemplation of their signlessness. Such pronouncements reflect the dharma of the supreme meaning.

Even when perceiving signlessness [from the standpoint of the supreme meaning], one still refrains from relinquishing the great compassion or the great kindness employed in relation to beings. Rather one longs for that day when he will be able to instigate beings to become aware of the dharma of the supreme meaning?

---

165 – Making Offerings of Dharma Is Superior to Giving Every Gift to the Buddha

As for that which is superior even to using every sort of gift
In making offerings to the Buddha, the Bhagavān,
What sort of action might that be?
This refers specifically to making offerings of Dharma.

AV What sort of gift would be superior to offering to all śrāvaka-disciples, pratyekabuddhas, bodhisattvas, and buddhas all manner of flowers, fragrances, garlands, powdered incenses, lantern wheels, canopies, banners, pennants, music, medicines, fine foods and beverages, and other such things?

The reply indicates that this would be an offering of Dharma. Now what other aspect might such a Dharma offering possess?

---

166 – Upholding the Bodhisattva Canon Is the Foremost Dharma Offering

If one upholds the Bodhisattva Canon,
Even to the point of gaining realization of the *dhāraṇīs*—
If one enters into and reaches the bottom of Dharma's source—
This is what constitutes the offering of Dharma.

AV If one is to conform in this to the Bodhisattva canon, [one should contemplate the following ideas from the *Vimalakīrti Sutra*]:

"The sutras spoken by the Tathāgata and the other scriptures are extremely profound in their clarification of the characteristics of dharmas. They are diametrically opposed to the ways of the world. It is difficult to succeed in reaching to the very bottom of them. It is difficult to perceive the subtleties involved in the ultimate meaning of being free of attachment.

"[That which is included in the Bodhisattva canon] is such as receives the seal of certification of the seal described in the *King of Dhāraṇīs Sutra*. It explains that the causes for realizing irreversibility are born from the six perfections. [The Bodhisattva canon] skillfully subsumes what should be subsumed. It complies with and enters into the dharmas equipping one for bodhi. It brings one into unity with the nature of the right enlightenment. It enters into all forms of the great compassion and discourses on the great kindness.

"It abandons the many demonic views, skillfully explains conditioned arising, and enters into the sphere of the nonexistence of beings, the nonexistence of a life, the nonexistence of any developing entity, and the nonexistence of persons. It accords with emptiness, signlessness, wishlessness, and non-production.

"It leads one to sit at the site where bodhi is realized and set in motion the wheel of Dharma whereupon one is praised by the gods, dragons, *yakṣas*, and *gandharvas*. It delivers one from the mire of the householder's life and draws one in among the Āryas. It expounds on all of the bodhisattva practices and enters into the eloquence consisting of [being unobstructed in understanding] dharmas, in realizing their meanings, in formulating articulate phrasing, and in speaking about them with delight.

"It shakes the world with the thunder of that sound which proclaims impermanence, suffering, absence of self, and other such dharmas. It strikes terror into all who subscribe to the attachments to views and attainments characteristic of the non-Buddhist treatises. It is praised by all buddhas. It counteracts one's coursing in cyclic existence and reveals the bliss of nirvāṇa. If one explains, if one upholds, if one analytically investigates, and if one adopts sutras such as these, it is this which qualifies as the offering of Dharma."

Additionally, those who give offerings of Dharma succeed in achieving irreversibility and thus do not fall, this on account of the *dhāraṇīs* which follow along with them [from life to life, guarding them] in their practice. In those profound dharmas which correspond to emptiness, signlessness, wishlessness, and non-production, one enters and reaches to their very bottom where one remains unmoving and free of doubts. It is this which qualifies as the offering of the dharma of the most supreme meaning.

TN Bhikshu Vaśitva's long passage which I have enclosed in quotes (consisting of all but the last paragraph immediately above) is his paraphrase of Medicine King Buddha in the "Dharma Offerings" chapter of the *Vimalakīrti Sutra*. (See T14.475.556b–c and T14.476.586b–c for the Kumārajīva and Xuanzang translations.)

167 – Rely on Meaning, Not Flavors; Enter the Profound Path, Avoiding Negligence
One should rely upon the meaning. One must not cherish only the various flavors. In the Path of the profound Dharma One enters with skill and must not fall prey to negligence.

AV Additionally, as for this making of offerings of Dharma, whether it be in the meditative reflection on dharmas or in the implementation of dharmas in one's practice, whether it be in acting in accord with conditioned arising, whether it be in the abandonment of views seizing on extremes, whether it be in the realization whereby one never leaves the unproduced-dharmas patience, whether it be in gaining entry to the nonexistence of the self, whether it be in remaining free of any opposing, struggling, or disputation in the midst of the circumstances formed by causes and conditions, or whether it be in the abandonment of the self and anything belonging to a self—in all such circumstances, one should rely upon the meaning. One must not be motivated by an affection which chases after the flavor of the various forms of decorous phrasing.

One should rely upon wisdom and must not merely rely upon impressions gained through one's consciousnesses. One should rely upon ultimate-meaning scriptures and must not become attached to worldly and common discourses which do not reflect the ultimate meaning. One should rely upon Dharma and must not seize upon the views which people hold. In one's practice, one should accord with and follow those dharmas which correspond to reality, thus entering into that place wherein there is no abiding.

One should skillfully contemplate the cycle of ignorance, karmic compositional factors, consciousness, name-and-form, the six sense faculties, contact, feeling, craving, grasping, becoming, birth, aging, death, sorrow, lamentation, suffering-laden afflictions, and the very extremes of difficulty—perceiving them all as abiding in a state of complete cessation. After one has contemplated the circumstances of conditioned arising in this manner, one may draw upon it endlessly and, on account of remaining sympathetically mindful of beings, one refrains from becoming attached to any views and refrains from falling into negligence.

If one is able to constantly act in this manner, then and only then does this qualify as an offering of the unsurpassed Dharma.

TN Bhikshu Vaśitva continues here his paraphrasing of ideas from the *Vimalakīrti Sutra*. One will note his encouragement to hew to the dictates of the four reliances with respect to Dharma together with his counsel on transcendence-based contemplation of the twelve-linked causal chain. It is through such an elevated perspective and perception that one is able to draw forth endless compassion as one works for the liberation of countless beings trapped in karma-bound suffering. It is through deep realization of this contemplation that one perceives the emptiness and intrinsically nirvāṇa-like nature of all that exists. It is by resort to contemplations of this sort that the Great Vehicle is able to proclaim the possibility of "sublime existence" even in the arena of cyclic births and deaths.

---

168 – Buddhahood is Gained by Cultivating the Provisions in Countless Future Lives

One cultivates these provisions in this manner
For kalpas as numerous as the Ganges' sands,
Doing so sometimes as a monastic, sometimes as a householder.
Thus one will succeed in perfecting the right enlightenment.

AV One cultivates the provisions in accordance with the preceding explanations, doing so for a Ganges' sands number of great kalpas. One does so within the monastic communities and householder communities of the Bodhisattva Vehicle. It is over a long period of time that one fulfills one's vows and then finally succeeds in realizing the right enlightenment.

I present this based on those stanzas about the provisions
To stimulate contemplative reflections about bodhi.
As their portrayal of the provisions' meaning is already flawless.
The aim here was merely to be able to accord with those verses.

My present analysis of those stanzas
May have either enhanced or detracted from their meanings.
Where the explanation has well matched the verses' meanings,
I pray the wisdom of the Worthies will acquiesce in it.

May any meritorious goodness I might have created
Through explaining those verses devoted to the provisions
Be dedicated to the beings coursing on in cyclic existence
That they may gain the right and universal awakening.

The End of Ārya Nāgārjuna's *Treatise on the Provisions for Enlightenment.*

The End of the Explanation Set Forth by Me, Bhikshu Vaśitva.

ABOUT THE TRANSLATOR

Bhikshu Dharmamitra (ordination name "Heng Shou" – 釋恆授) is a Chinese-tradition translator-monk and one of the early American disciples (since 1968) of the late Weiyang Ch'an patriarch, Dharma teacher, and exegete, the Venerable Master Hsuan Hua (宣化上人). He has a total of 23 years in robes during two periods as a monastic (1969–1975; 1991 to present).

Dharmamitra's principal educational foundations as a translator lie in four years of intensive monastic training and Chinese-language study of classic Mahāyāna texts in a small-group setting under Master Hua from 1968–1972, undergraduate Chinese language study at Portland State University, a year of intensive one-on-one Classical Chinese study at the Fu Jen University Language Center near Taipei, and two years at the University of Washington's School of Asian Languages and Literature (1988–90).

Since taking robes again under Master Hua in 1991, Dharmamitra has devoted his energies primarily to study and translation of classic Mahāyāna texts with a special interest in works by Ārya Nāgārjuna and related authors. To date, he has translated a dozen important texts, most of which are slated for publication by Kalavinka Press.

Kalavinka Buddhist Classics Title List

Meditation Instruction Texts

The Essentials of Buddhist Meditation
A marvelously complete classic *śamathā-vipaśyanā* (calming-and-insight) meditation manual. By Tiantai Śramaṇa Zhiyi (538–597 CE).

The Six Gates to the Sublime
The earliest Indian Buddhist meditation method explaining the essentials of breath and calming-and-insight meditation. By Śramaṇa Zhiyi.

Bodhisattva Path Texts

Nāgārjuna on the Six Perfections
Chapters 17–30 of Ārya Nāgārjuna's *Mahāprajñāpāramitā Upadeśa*.

Marvelous Stories from the Perfection of Wisdom
130 stories from Ārya Nāgārjuna's *Mahāprajñāpāramitā Upadeśa*.

A Strand of Dharma Jewels (Ārya Nāgārjuna's *Ratnāvalī*)
The earliest extant edition, translated by Paramārtha: *ca* 550 CE

Nāgārjuna's Guide to the Bodhisattva Path
The *Bodhisaṃbhāra Treatise* with abridged Vaśitva commentary.

The Bodhisaṃbhāra Treatise Commentary
The complete exegesis by the Indian Bhikshu Vaśitva (*ca* 300–500 CE).

Letter from a Friend - The Three Earliest Editions
The earliest extant editions of Ārya Nāgārjuna's *Suhṛlekkha*:

Translated by Tripiṭaka Master Guṇavarman	(*ca* 425 CE)
Translated by Tripiṭaka Master Saṅghavarman	(*ca* 450 CE)
Translated by Tripiṭaka Master Yijing	(*ca* 675 CE)

Resolve-for-Enlightenment Texts

On Generating the Resolve to Become a Buddha
On the Resolve to Become a Buddha by Ārya Nāgārjuna
Exhortation to Resolve on Buddhahood by Patriarch Sheng'an Shixian
Exhortation to Resolve on Buddhahood by the Tang Literatus, Peixiu

Vasubandhu's Treatise on the Bodhisattva Vow
By Vasubandhu Bodhisattva (*ca* 300 CE)

*All Kalavinka Press translations include facing-page source text.

Printed in the USA
CPSIA information can be obtained
at www.ICGtesting.com
LVHW041115061023
760352LV00017BA/68